INDIGENOUS RULES OF ENGAGEMENT

The Definitive Guide to First Nations Engagement in Australia

SHANNON BEST

First published 2026

Big Sky Publishing Pty Ltd
PO Box 303, Newport, NSW 2106, Australia
Phone: 1300 364 611
Fax: (61 2) 9918 2396
Email: info@bigskypublishing.com.au
Web: www.bigskypublishing.com.au

A catalogue record for this book is available from the National Library of Australia

Title: Indigenous Rules of Engagement
ISBN: 9781923514461

INDIGENOUS RULES OF ENGAGEMENT

The Definitive Guide to First Nations Engagement in Australia

www.bigskypublishing.com.au

SHANNON BEST

Contents

PART 3
CULTIVATING RESPECTFUL RELATIONSHIPS

PART 4
TOWARDS RECONCILIATION

Acknowledgments

This book is dedicated to my family. Everything I do is tied to them, and to the strength and grounding they've given me throughout my life.

To my big brother, Hague — thank you for helping me navigate spaces that can be challenging at times. Your guidance, calm perspective and steady support continue to make a real difference.

To my mother, Ysola — although you passed in 2007, your influence has never left me. You laid the groundwork that shaped who I am and, through osmosis, instilled my drive, my pride, and my responsibility to continue preserving our culture. Your presence remains in every step I take.

To my extended family — I'm grateful for the time we share and the way your company keeps me centred. You remind me of where I come from and why this work matters.

And to the friends whose support has travelled with me across years and continents — Jimmy S, Greg K, Edward M and Dave B — thank you for the loyalty, encouragement and friendship that continue today.

To all of you: thank you for shaping my journey and standing with me as I carry this work forward.

Foreword

As the President of the Kombumerri Aboriginal Corporation for Culture, I am proud to support *Indigenous Rules of Engagement* by Shannon Best, is an important and timely contribution to the conversation around how to respectfully and appropriately engage with our communities.

Shannon has worked tirelessly across many sectors to elevate Aboriginal voices, support our cultural practices, and protect our knowledge. His experience, both lived and professional, has been brought together in this book with great care and purpose.

This work offers insight for those seeking to understand the expectations and responsibilities that come with working with Aboriginal people. It sets out, in plain terms, what respectful engagement should look like, and challenges some of the tokenistic approaches we still see today.

While this book will not and cannot speak for all communities, it provides a valuable guide, especially here in South East Queensland, where our people continue to lead in cultural knowledge, language, and advocacy.

On behalf of KACC, I commend this book to all who are serious about learning, listening, and doing things the right way.

Mathew O'Connor,
President
Kombumerri Aboriginal Corporation for Culture (KACC)

Jimbelungare

Friendship/relationship

Authors Note

Australia is home to extraordinary cultural and linguistic diversity, with more than 250 distinct Aboriginal and Torres Strait Islander language groups and over 800 dialects spoken before colonisation. Each language carries its own law, history, identity, and relationship to Country.

My family are Traditional Owners from South-East Queensland, and the language spoken across our Country is Yugambeh. Our Elders and knowledge-holders, including members of my own family, have committed decades to researching, teaching, and revitalising our language, culture, and history. Their dedication has helped ensure Yugambeh knowledge endures for future generations.

Like many First Nations peoples, our language, cultural practices, and histories were suppressed following the arrival of settlers. Despite this, our people have continued to maintain and reclaim cultural knowledge with resilience and pride.

Throughout this book, I have included selected words and reflections to help readers better understand my background, my family, and the influences that shaped my decision to write this work. These inclusions are shared with respect to my community and ancestors, and to offer a small window into the lived experiences and cultural grounding that inform my perspective. In doing so, I honour the Yugambeh language and worldview — Kunga — listen — inviting readers to pause, reflect, and walk beside our story rather than simply observe it.

This book is written with deep respect for all Aboriginal and Torres Strait Islander nations and languages across this continent. While my perspective is grounded in my Yugambeh heritage and community experience, I acknowledge the rich diversity across our lands and recognise the strength and authority of each community in holding and sharing its own cultural knowledge.

Who This Book Is For

Indigenous Rules of Engagement is written primarily for non-Indigenous individuals and organisations who are seeking to work respectfully and effectively with Aboriginal and Torres Strait Islander peoples in Australia. It offers guidance for those in government, planning, education, the arts, infrastructure, and community services—particularly those whose decisions and actions impact Indigenous communities, culture, and Country. This book is for:

- **Engagement officers, policy advisors, consultants, and program managers** seeking ethical, culturally informed approaches to engagement.

- **Professionals** responsible for designing and delivering projects on or impacting Aboriginal land and communities.
- **Researchers, educators, and cultural heritage specialists** striving to embed Indigenous perspectives in their work.
- **New staff** entering Indigenous engagement roles who need practical guidance and cultural grounding.
- **Allies** who want to support Indigenous peoples with integrity and clarity of purpose.

While it is written from an Australian context, we acknowledge that many readers may identify as Indigenous in the countries or territories from which their ancestors came. We recognise the diverse global definitions and expressions of Indigeneity, as well as the shared histories of colonisation, cultural resilience, and the ongoing struggle for recognition.

However, this guide does not attempt to speak on behalf of Aboriginal and Torres Strait Islander peoples. Instead, it is a resource for those outside these communities to better understand the responsibilities of engaging with them. At its core, this book is about respect, relationship-building, and the long-term work of walking alongside, not ahead or behind.

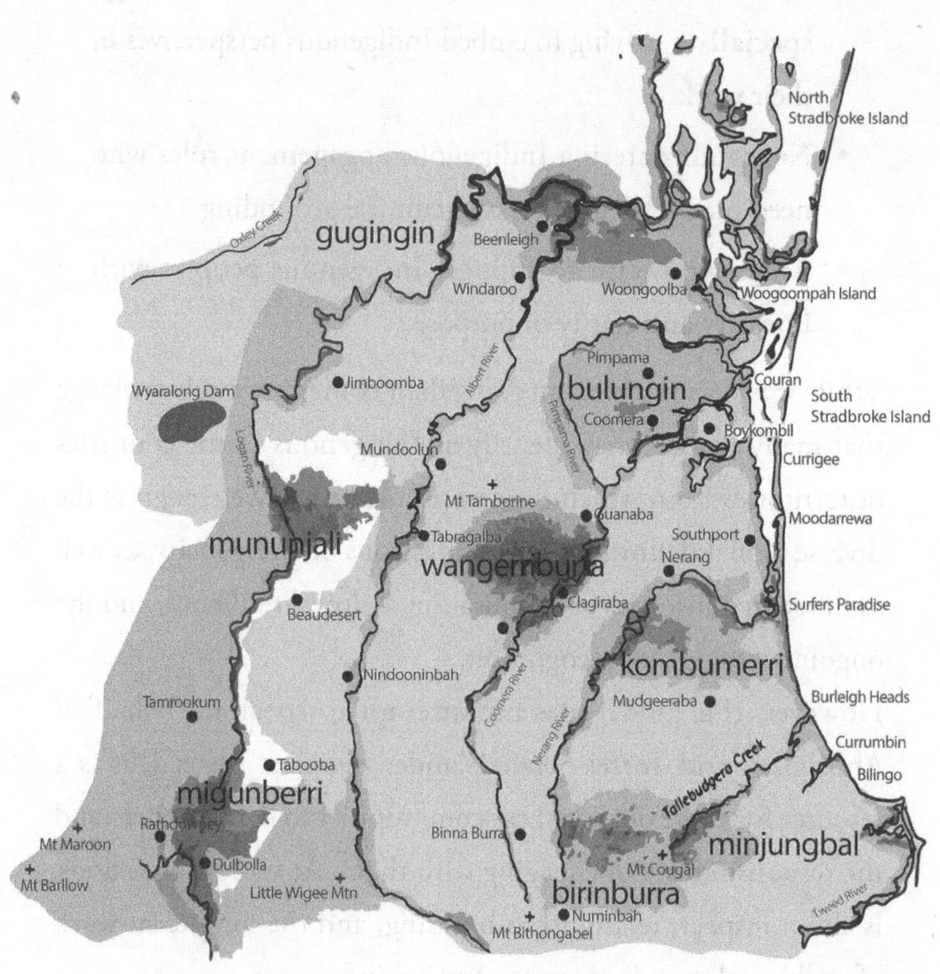

North Stradbroke Island
Oxley Creek
gugingin
Beenleigh
Windaroo
Woongoolba
Woogoompah Island
Pimpama
Jimboomba
Albert River
bulungin
Couran
South Stradbroke Island
Wyaralong Dam
Logan River
Coomera
Boykombil
Pimpama River
Mundoolun
Currigee
Mt Tamborine
Guanaba
Moodarrewa
Tabragalba
Southport
mununjali
wangerriburra
Nerang
Clagiraba
Beaudesert
Surfers Paradise
kombumerri
Nindooninbah
Coomera River
Mudgeeraba
Tamrookum
Nerang River
Burleigh Heads
Currumbin
Tabooba
Tallebudgera Creek
Bilingo
migunberri
Rathdowney
Mt Maroon
Binna Burra
minjungbal
Mt Cougal
Dulbolla
Mt Barllow
Little Wigee Mtn
birinburra
Tweed River
Numinbah
Mt Bithongabel

Yugambeh Language

The Yugambeh Language is one of the First Languages of South-East Queensland. It is part of the wider Yugambeh-Bundjalung language family and has been spoken across the region for thousands of generations. Yugambeh Country stretches from the Logan River in the north, across the Gold Coast, to the Tweed River in the south, and west toward the Scenic Rim.

Yugambeh holds cultural law, place-names, stories, kinship ties, and knowledge of Country. It is a living language, carried by Elders, families, and community, and continues to be spoken, taught, and revitalised today. Its ongoing use reflects the enduring presence, authority, and cultural sovereignty of the Yugambeh people on their land.

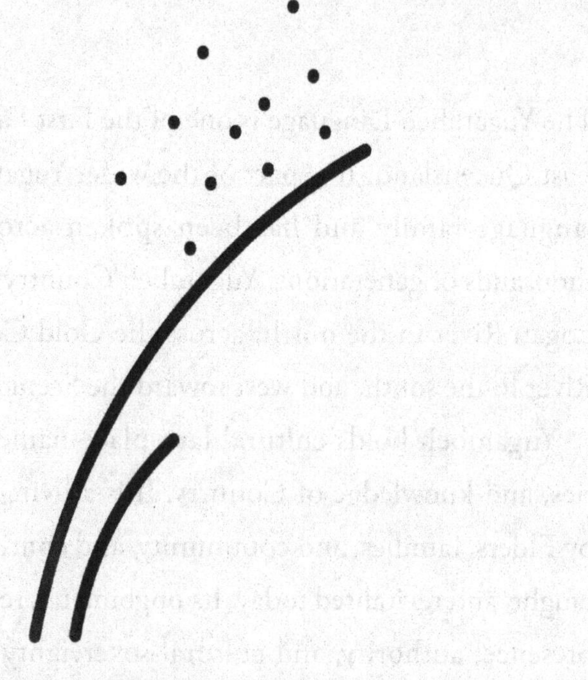
bareibunn

Introduction

In a world where the need for genuine understanding and respect across cultures has never been more critical, *Indigenous Rules of Engagement* serves as a timely and essential resource. This guide stems from a journey shaped by the complexities of working in government, where I witnessed firsthand how well-intentioned actions, when lacking cultural depth and consideration, can lead to unintended harm. It is born out of the desire to bridge the gap between good intentions and respectful, effective engagement with Indigenous communities.

This book is not merely a manual but a navigator for those seeking to collaborate meaningfully, honouring the histories, cultures, and spirits of Indigenous peoples. It reframes the notion of "rules" not as rigid directives but as flexible insights, woven from lived experiences within Indigenous communities and practical applications in professional spaces. Structured to reflect strategies and philosophies tested and refined over years of work, this guide offers tools to foster understanding, build relationships, and create spaces for authentic connection.

Central to this guide is the principle of "Nothing About Us Without Us." This philosophy underscores the critical need for Indigenous peoples to actively participate in decisions and initiatives that affect their lives. Effective engagement is not about speaking on behalf of Indigenous communities but empowering their voices and perspectives in meaningful ways. Through the chapters that follow, this book delves into the importance of cultural competency—an understanding of history, traditions, and contemporary realities—as the foundation for respectful and impactful engagement.

This book is an invitation to approach Indigenous engagement with an open heart and an eager mind. Whether you are new to this space or seeking to deepen your practices, the perspectives shared here aim to enrich your journey. Each chapter offers a blend of practical strategies and reflective insights to navigate the complexities of engagement while building respectful, enduring relationships.

The Inspiration Behind the Book

My transition into a government role was an eye-opening experience that served as the catalyst for this book. Recognising the gaps and challenges in Indigenous engagement motivated me to create a resource to help others navigate this space effectively. On a personal level, this book is deeply rooted in my experiences as an Aboriginal person witnessing the daily impacts of colonisation, including the harm inflicted on my culture, family, and community.

I recognise that most people engaging in this space act with the best intentions. However, without cultural knowledge or adherence to proper protocols, even well-meaning actions can lead to complications or further harm. This book is my effort to share the lessons I have learned, offering guidance to help others engage thoughtfully and respectfully with Indigenous communities.

The Essence of the Title

The title *Indigenous Rules of Engagement* was chosen to capture attention and convey the book's purpose effectively. While the word "rules" may imply a rigid framework, this book is anything but prescriptive. Instead, it offers suggestions and insights to guide engagement efforts, recognising the fluid and nuanced nature of working with Indigenous communities. These are not commandments to follow but a compass to help navigate the challenges of fostering genuine relationships.

Structuring Our Journey

The structure of this book mirrors the approach I used in my professional roles within engagement. It is organised to reflect strategies and philosophies that have proven effective in building meaningful connections and achieving shared goals. While my focus has been on my own Traditional area, the approaches outlined here are adaptable and can guide engagement efforts in other parts of the country.

This structure allows readers to explore the foundational principles of Indigenous engagement, gain practical tools for building relationships, and reflect on how to foster inclusive, effective partnerships. The book is designed to serve both newcomers and seasoned professionals looking to refine their practices.

Recognising the Gap

One of the most striking observations during my time in local government was the glaring void in Indigenous engagement. What seemed straightforward to me — consulting communities, following protocols, and listening to Elders — was often perceived as an insurmountable challenge by others. Recognising this gap, I spearheaded the development of an engagement program tailored for council use. Its success was not mine alone but the result of collaboration with dedicated professionals who exemplified the power of teamwork in achieving meaningful outcomes.

This experience reaffirmed the importance of equipping people with the knowledge and tools to engage respectfully and effectively. This book is an extension of that work, designed to empower readers to bridge the gap between intention and action.

The Importance of Cultural Competency

Engaging with Indigenous communities requires more than a checklist; it demands a deep understanding of their history, culture, and language. Cultural competency is not just beneficial; it is essential. However, it is important to approach engagement with realistic expectations. Often, Indigenous engagement is initiated by external entities rather than by the community itself.

There isn't a group of Elders sitting around a campfire, waiting to bestow cultural wisdom on someone's "Ten-Year Greening Plan" or another project. Respectful engagement requires effort, humility, and a willingness to learn on the part of those initiating the process.

This book invites readers to approach Indigenous engagement with openness, respect, and a commitment to continuous learning. Through its pages, I hope to inspire meaningful, inclusive, and impactful collaborations that honour the strength and diversity of Indigenous communities.

Ina

To listen quietly / rest; pause to understand before acting

PART 1

UNDERSTANDING THE FOUNDATIONS

gwong gubung
water hole

1

The Starting Point

Acknowledging Australia's History

Engaging with Aboriginal communities begins not with action, but with understanding, and that understanding must start with the truth. Colonisation in Australia did not end with settlement. It is not a chapter of history we have moved beyond. Colonisation is ongoing. Its impacts are still being felt through policy, planning, dispossession, and systemic exclusion.

Colonisation in Australia was marked by coordinated and systemic acts of violence, forced removals, cultural suppression, and legal exclusion. Aboriginal and Torres Strait Islander peoples were removed from their lands, cutting the connection to Country that forms the foundation of identity, spirituality, governance, and law.

The establishment of missions and government reserves, coupled with protection and assimilation policies, sought to dismantle Aboriginal autonomy and erase cultural practices. These actions were not isolated or accidental; they were coordinated, systemic, and resourced through formal government policy and funding. Their purpose was control, containment, and erasure.

One critical but often overlooked part of this history is the deliberate transformation of Aboriginal people into a labour force, usually unpaid, underpaid, or coerced. On pastoral stations, in domestic service, on missions, and through child removal, Aboriginal people were positioned as a cheap and compliant workforce to serve colonial industries and households. Wages were withheld, movement was restricted, and consent was rarely sought. These were not unfortunate by-products of colonisation; they were central features of it.

The legacy of these actions lives on today. Intergenerational trauma, social and economic disadvantage, and mistrust of institutions are not accidents. They are the direct outcomes of a system designed to dispossess, control, and exploit.

For many Australians, confronting this history is complex. It disrupts the national narrative of peaceful settlement and reveals the deep structural inequalities that persist. But facing this truth is necessary not just to understand the resilience of Aboriginal communities, but to begin rebuilding relationships grounded in honesty and respect.

Respectful engagement requires more than acknowledgement. It demands recognition of the ongoing impacts of colonisation and a willingness to engage with communities with humility and accountability. Without this, engagement risks becoming superficial, tokenistic, or even harmful.

Recognising the Complexity of Aboriginal Heritage

Australia is home to the world's oldest living cultures, with extraordinary diversity in language, law, knowledge systems, and governance. Before colonisation, over 250 language groups and more than 800 dialects existed, each tied to specific territories and cultural responsibilities.

These groups were and remain sovereign Nations. They are not a single culture or community. Each Nation holds its own governance structures, ancestral connections, and obligations to Country. These systems continue to define rights, responsibilities, and relationships within and between communities today.

Engaging with Aboriginal peoples requires moving beyond generalised assumptions. It requires a commitment to understanding the specific community or Nation you are working with, their history, their cultural protocols, and their contemporary realities. It also requires recognition of the roles of Elders and knowledge holders in guiding decisions and upholding cultural authority.

Too often, engagement efforts fail because they treat Aboriginal peoples as a homogenous group. This not only misrepresents the diversity of Aboriginal heritage but risks undermining trust and excluding the very people whose voices are essential. Respectful engagement honours the uniqueness of each Nation, while recognising the collective strength Aboriginal peoples share in surviving ongoing colonisation.

The richness of Aboriginal heritage is not something to acknowledge in passing; it is something to actively learn from. It holds knowledge that can guide better ways to care for land, govern relationships, and build community. Embracing this complexity is not a challenge; it is an opportunity for deeper understanding and mutual growth.

The Principle of "Nothing About Us Without Us"

The principle of "Nothing About Us Without Us" is not just a slogan; it is a fundamental framework for ethical and practical engagement. It demands inclusion, respect, and recognition of Aboriginal leadership and self-determination.

For most of Australia's colonial and post-colonial history, Aboriginal peoples were excluded from decisions that directly affected their lives, lands, and communities. Policies were created and enforced without consent, cultural context, or understanding, and the consequences were often devastating.

This principle calls for a reversal of that practice. It means that Aboriginal peoples must be at the centre of decision-making processes that impact them, not consulted after the fact but involved from the outset. This includes planning, implementation, evaluation, and governance. It also recognises that consultation alone is not enough; engagement must be genuine, respectful, and led by those with cultural authority.

Aboriginal peoples are the experts on their own lives, cultures, and futures. Recognising this is not just an ethical position; it is a practical necessity. Projects and initiatives that do not include

Aboriginal voices are less likely to succeed and more likely to cause harm. Respecting "Nothing About Us Without Us" is not only about inclusion, but it is also about legitimacy, relevance, and responsibility.

Laying the Groundwork

The starting point for any engagement with Aboriginal communities must rest on three interdependent truths:

- That colonisation is ongoing, and its impacts are deeply embedded in contemporary systems and experiences;
- That Aboriginal cultures are diverse, sovereign, and resilient, requiring tailored, Nation-specific engagement approaches; and
- That decisions about Aboriginal lives and lands must be guided by those who hold the cultural and legal authority to speak for them.

This is not about what we do for communities; it is about how we work with them. With respect. With humility. And with a willingness to listen and learn.

These foundational understandings are not a preface to the real work of engagement; they are the work. The chapters ahead will build on these principles to guide respectful, honest, and effective engagement with Aboriginal peoples and their Countries.

ballun

river

2

Understanding Aboriginal Identity

The Australian Government's Definition

In discussions of engagement with Aboriginal communities, understanding the formal definition of Aboriginal identity is a critical starting point. The Australian Government's recognition of an Aboriginal person is based on three interrelated criteria:

- **Descent:** The individual must be of Aboriginal or Torres Strait Islander descent.
- **Self-identification:** The individual must identify as an Aboriginal or Torres Strait Islander.
- **Community acceptance:** The individual must be accepted as Aboriginal or Torres Strait Islander by the community in which they live or have lived.

This definition acknowledges that Aboriginal identity is not merely a matter of ancestry or biology. It also reflects cultural and communal dimensions, recognising that identity is affirmed through lived experience and acceptance by the broader community.

The Role of Descent, Self-Identification, and Community Acceptance

Each of the three criteria serves a distinct purpose:

- **Descent** provides the genealogical link to Aboriginal ancestors. It ties individuals to their cultural heritage and historical lineage.
- **Self-identification** reflects the individual's personal recognition of their Aboriginal identity. This criterion respects individuals' right to embrace their heritage and assert their place within the community.
- **Community acceptance** underscores the collective aspect of Aboriginal identity. It ensures that individuals are recognised by the community as belonging, reflecting the interconnected nature of Aboriginal culture.

These three components work together to balance personal, cultural, and social dimensions of identity, ensuring that recognition is holistic and meaningful.

Why Identity is Central to Engagement

Understanding the formal definition of Aboriginal identity is crucial for meaningful engagement. It challenges superficial or reductive assumptions about what it means to be Aboriginal and emphasises the need for context-sensitive approaches.

Engagement efforts often involve navigating diverse identities within Aboriginal communities. People may identify in different ways based on their connection to Country, family, or cultural practices. Respecting these nuances ensures that engagement is inclusive and representative of the community as a whole.

The principle of **community acceptance** also underscores the importance of broad community consultation. Engagement should not be limited to a single person or group but should involve dialogue with a wide range of voices to capture the diversity of perspectives.

Identity and Cultural Protocols

The interplay of descent, self-identification, and community acceptance also informs cultural protocols, which are essential for respectful engagement. Understanding who holds cultural authority within a community, whether Elders, leaders, or knowledge keepers, requires an awareness of these criteria. By respecting identity and its complexities, engagement can build trust and foster genuine collaboration.

The Australian Government's definition of an Aboriginal person provides a framework for understanding identity that is both inclusive and multidimensional. It recognises that being Aboriginal is not just about ancestry but also about cultural belonging and community recognition.

For those engaging with Aboriginal communities, this definition serves as a reminder to approach identity with respect and sensitivity. By understanding and honouring these aspects of identity, we can create spaces for more meaningful, inclusive, and effective partnerships.

3

Understanding Key Terminology

Engaging respectfully with Aboriginal and Torres Strait Islander peoples requires more than good intentions; it requires accuracy. Language matters. The terms we use shape how we understand roles, responsibilities, and authority. In the context of land, culture, and community, terminology is not just about preference; it reflects deep histories, legal realities, and cultural protocols.

This chapter explains three commonly used terms — Traditional Owner, Traditional Custodian, and First Nations — and clarifies their meanings, distinctions, and appropriate uses. Misusing or interchanging these terms can cause confusion, undermine trust, or misrepresent cultural authority. Getting them right is a foundational step toward meaningful engagement.

Traditional Owner

Traditional Owner refers to Aboriginal people who hold cultural, spiritual, and familial responsibilities to a specific area of land or water. These responsibilities are inherited through kinship systems and guided by lore, ceremony, and ancestral knowledge. Traditional Owners are not simply people with a connection to Country; they are those who are lawfully and culturally bound to it.

This role includes obligations to protect sacred sites, maintain stories and languages, uphold cultural protocols, and speak for Country when decisions are being made. These responsibilities are lifelong, intergenerational, and non-transferable. They are not chosen; they are carried.

In some cases, Traditional Owners are recognised through formal legal frameworks such as the *Native Title Act 1993* or the *Aboriginal Land Rights Act 1983*. However, legal recognition does not define cultural authority. Many Traditional Owners continue to exercise their responsibilities without statutory recognition, and that authority remains valid and respected within the community.

Traditional Owners play a central role in matters relating to land use, cultural heritage, environmental management, and planning processes. Their voices are essential, not only because of their cultural knowledge but because of the legal and moral authority they hold over their Country.

Traditional Custodian

The term Traditional Custodian appears in some public-facing communications, particularly in the arts, education, or community events. However, it is not a term recognised in legislation or formal government policy and should not be confused with Traditional Owner.

In some cultural contexts, individuals may describe themselves as custodians of particular knowledge, stories, or responsibilities. This reflects an internal community role, but it is not a substitute for the status of Traditional Owner, nor does it carry legal standing.

Importantly, this term should not be confused with custodial ownership, which refers to arrangements in which governments or legal entities hold land or assets on behalf of Aboriginal groups through specific mechanisms. Custodial ownership is a legal concept. Traditional Custodian is not.

While some individuals may identify as custodians in culturally appropriate ways, the term is not interchangeable with Traditional Owner, and its use—especially by external organisations—should be considered carefully. Where engagement or recognition is required, the appropriate approach is to ask individuals and communities how they identify and what terminology reflects their cultural and legal position.

First Nations

First Nations is a collective and political term that refers to the Aboriginal and Torres Strait Islander peoples of Australia. It highlights their sovereignty, cultural distinctiveness, and status as the original peoples of this continent.

The term recognises that there is not one Indigenous culture, but many Nations, each with its own language, law, customs, and Country. First Nations also reflect a shared experience of colonisation, dispossession, and resilience. It is a term often used in advocacy, national policy discussions, and education to centre Indigenous voices and self-determination.

Unlike Traditional Owner, which is specific to a person's relationship with a defined area of Country, First Nations refers to a collective identity. A person may identify as First Nations without being a Traditional Owner of the land they currently live on, particularly in cases of historical displacement, removal, or migration.

The term is powerful and inclusive, but it should not be used in place of locally specific recognition. Where decisions affect a particular place, identifying and engaging with the relevant Traditional Owners remains essential.

Distinctions and Overlaps

While both terms—Traditional Owner and First Nations—are important, they serve different purposes and highlight various aspects of Aboriginal identity and governance.

- **Traditional Owner** is specific and localised, referring to individuals or groups with ancestral ties to a particular area. It carries responsibilities connected to land care and cultural heritage within that specific region.
- **First Nations** is broader and collective, encompassing all Aboriginal and Torres Strait Islander peoples. It underscores the shared experiences and sovereignty of Indigenous Australians as a whole.

The two terms often overlap in practice. A Traditional Owner is also part of a First Nation, and their responsibilities to their land contribute to the collective identity of their Nation. However, not all First Nations people are Traditional Owners of the land they live on, especially if they reside outside their ancestral Country.

Why Accurate Terminology is Essential for Engagement

Using accurate terminology is crucial for respectful and effective engagement. Misusing terms like Traditional Owner or First Nations can cause confusion or inadvertently exclude certain groups. For example:

- Referring to someone as a Traditional Owner when they are not can undermine community dynamics or misrepresent authority.
- Using First Nations when referring to a specific Traditional Owner group may dilute the localised nature of cultural and legal connections to land.

Understanding these distinctions helps ensure that engagement efforts are targeted, inclusive, and culturally appropriate. It also demonstrates respect for the unique identities, rights, and responsibilities of Indigenous Australians.

Words shape the foundation of engagement. Getting them right is the first step to walking respectfully.

What This Means in Practice

The terms Traditional Owner and First Nations are more than labels; they are expressions of identity, sovereignty, and cultural connection. Recognising the distinctions and overlaps between these terms is fundamental to fostering respectful relationships and meaningful partnerships with Aboriginal communities.

By understanding and using these terms correctly, we honour the diversity and richness of Aboriginal cultures while ensuring that engagement efforts are grounded in cultural and historical accuracy. This understanding lays the foundation for building trust and collaboration in all aspects of Indigenous engagement.

gaia

Hunt

4

Understanding Country – More Than Just Place

What Is Country?

In Aboriginal and Torres Strait Islander worldviews, Country is not just land. It is not simply a landscape, a property, or a place on a map. Country is a living, breathing entity that holds spiritual, cultural, social, and ecological meaning. It includes land, waters, skies, seasons, plants, animals, people, and ancestral beings. It holds law, ceremony, language, and memory.

Country is home, law, kin, and teacher. It is both identity and responsibility.

This relationship is reciprocal: Aboriginal peoples do not simply live *on* Country, they live *with* and *through* it. In turn, Country sustains, instructs, and relies upon its people. There is no separation between self and land. The health of Country and the health of people are one and the same.

Country Is Not Just a Feeling of Home

Many non-Indigenous people speak of feeling a strong personal attachment to a place, perhaps their home, their block of land, a beach they've visited for decades, or a town where generations of family have lived. These connections are valid, meaningful, and often deeply felt.

However, they are not the same as an Aboriginal person's connection to Country.

Personal attachments tend to develop over a lifetime, sometimes across several generations, and are often emotional, experiential, or tied to memories of family and life events. By contrast, Aboriginal connection to Country is ancestral and legally, spiritually, and culturally embedded in systems of lore and governance that have existed for thousands of years.

This difference does not diminish anyone's experience, but it does ask non-Indigenous Australians to recognise that their connection to land is not equivalent to that of Traditional Owners.

Country Has Law, Lore, and Custodians

To understand Country, is to understand, that it is governed by its own laws and custodians. These laws are not merely about land ownership; they are frameworks of responsibility embedded in kinship systems, songlines, ceremonies, and cultural protocols. They are spiritual, legal, and practical all at once. These systems predate colonisation by thousands of generations and continue to shape how land is cared for, who has authority to speak for it, and how decisions must be made in accordance with ancestral teachings.

Custodianship is not ownership in the Western sense. It is an obligation. It is not optional, and it is not symbolic. People are born into Country and inherit enduring duties to protect, honour, and sustain its integrity. These responsibilities are intergenerational, sacred, and non-transferable. They are embedded in identity and expressed through practice. No title deed, leasehold, government tenure, or planning scheme can override or replace them. Attempts to do so misunderstand the nature of these responsibilities and often result in harm, not only to Country but to cultural continuity and community wellbeing.

When Aboriginal people speak for Country, they are doing so not out of sentiment, nostalgia, or protest, but out of duty. It is a cultural and spiritual obligation grounded in law and lore. Speaking for Country means holding knowledge, standing in truth, and being answerable to ancestors, future generations, and the land itself. It is not a role one can choose to take on, nor can it be conferred without proper lineage, ceremony, and community validation.

To engage respectfully with Aboriginal communities, it is critical to recognise that these structures of law and obligation still exist, are still followed, and must be acknowledged. Without this understanding, engagement risks being extractive, dismissive, or tokenistic, even when well-intentioned. Listening to the voices of those who are lawfully and culturally authorised to speak for Country is not a courtesy; it is a necessity.

Country Can Be Urban Too

A widespread misconception is that Aboriginal connection to Country only exists in remote, rural, or "untouched" landscapes. But Country is not defined by how undeveloped it appears. Country exists in the city just as it does in the bush. The built environment may have changed the surface, but it has not erased the deep cultural foundations beneath.

The Gold Coast is Kombumerri Country. This is not a symbolic or romanticised claim—it is a real, continuous, and lawful relationship that has endured through colonisation, urbanisation, and rapid development. Just as Brisbane remains Turrbal and Jagera Country, and Sydney remains Gadigal Country, the Gold Coast is still—and always has been—Aboriginal land.

The Gold Coast's urban sprawl is built on our gathering spots, our camp sites, and our bora rings. The supermarkets are built where our hunting grounds once fed families. Roads are laid over ancient pathways that connected clans, sites, and stories. These are not relics of a distant past—they are part of a living cultural landscape that continues to hold significance, even if it is no longer visible to most.

This sprawl does not extinguish our cultural connection to the land. It does not sever our responsibilities nor diminish our authority. Kombumerri people continue to fulfil their custodial roles, maintaining relationships with place, advocating for cultural heritage, and carrying the responsibilities handed down through generations. This is often done quietly, without fanfare or formal recognition, and in the face of persistent structural and social pressures.

Just because a place has roads, buildings, and infrastructure does not mean Aboriginal connection to that land has ended. Country is not passive or inert; it continues to call for care, protection, and respect. Our Elders still speak for it, still walk it, still know it. Our knowledge systems are mapped over this land just as clearly as any street grid.

If your work takes place in a city or suburb, it is still taking place on Aboriginal land. Engagement must reflect that reality. This means recognising the ongoing cultural authority of Traditional Owners, understanding the layered histories of the land beneath your feet, and involving the right people in decision-making. Urban Country still has law. It still has custodians. And it still requires respect.

Country Is Not a Backdrop, It's a Stakeholder

In many engagement processes, Country is reduced to a setting, a backdrop to development, a resource to be managed, or a "natural asset" to be measured. This approach is rooted in a Western, utilitarian worldview that disconnects land from its cultural and spiritual significance. It treats Country as an object to be used rather than a living entity to be respected.

Country is not silent. It has agency. It speaks through changes in the land, the movement of animals, the quality of water, and the shifting winds. It speaks through our Elders, our stories, our languages, and our laws. Country bears witness to what has happened, and it carries the impacts of what is done to it, good or bad. It is not a backdrop to decisions. It is central to them.

Meaningful cultural engagement requires more than simply asking, "Who are the Traditional Owners of this place?" It requires asking, "What does this place need?" and "How do we ensure that its voice is heard in this process?" When you consult with the right people, those who are culturally authorised to speak, you are not only seeking community input. You are engaging with Country itself.

Country is not a metaphor for the environment. It is not interchangeable with landscape or ecology. It is law, story, identity, and belonging. When Aboriginal people talk about Country hurting, healing, or being disrespected, it is not poetic language; it is a literal truth grounded in a reciprocal relationship with land, water, and spirit.

Whether you are working in infrastructure development, environmental planning, land use policy, or cultural heritage management, acknowledging Country as a stakeholder requires a fundamental shift in thinking. It means recognising that decisions cannot be made *about* Country without speaking *to* Country, and that speaking to Country means listening to those bound by its law and lore.

Respecting Country as a stakeholder is not about sentiment or symbolism. It is about accountability. It is about recognising that the land is not just where we build, but who we answer to.

Respecting Connection to Country in Practice

To engage respectfully with Aboriginal connection to Country, consider the following principles:

- Never assume equivalence between your attachment to a place and an Aboriginal person's custodianship.
- Recognise the cultural authority of those who speak for Country. This may include Elders, cultural custodians, or knowledge holders.
- Avoid token gestures. Acknowledging Country at the start of a meeting is not enough; ask what Country requires from your project.
- Understand boundaries. Not everyone can speak for every place. Different people have responsibilities for different areas, stories, and ceremonies.
- Include Country in decision-making. Engagement is not complete unless it accounts for how decisions affect Country and its custodians.

What This Means in Practice: Walk Lightly, Listen Deeply

Understanding Country requires more than knowledge, it demands a shift in mindset. It means unlearning the colonial idea that land is passive, that it can be owned, controlled, divided, or exploited without consequence. Country is not a commodity. It is a living system of relationships between people, landforms, waters, plants, animals, and spirit. It is not something we stand on, but something we are a part of.

This shift is not theoretical. It is practical. It requires moving from dominion to duty, from extraction to respect, from ownership to relationship. It means seeing Country not as property, but as kin, not as a blank canvas, but as a keeper of memory, law, and meaning.

To walk on Country is a privilege. Every step carries weight. Every site carries significance, whether it is visible or not. Some places are ceremonial. Some are resting places. Some are sites of sorrow. Some are places of renewal. None are empty.

To engage with those who speak for Country is a responsibility. Traditional Custodians carry knowledge that is not only cultural but legal, spiritual, and ecological. Their voices are not just perspectives to consider; they are sources of authority and insight that must guide decision-making. To ignore them is not just disrespectful, it is negligent.

So, walk lightly. Tread with awareness. Know that every place you stand has a story older than your presence on it, older than the maps that mark it, and older than the systems that seek to define it.

Listen deeply. Listen to the land. Listen to those who are bound to it through law, lore, and lineage. In that listening, you may begin to understand that genuine engagement with Country is not about inclusion or consultation, it is about respect, responsibility, and relationship.

That is where all meaningful engagement begins.

5

Controlled by the Acts

The Historical Impact of Government Policies

The experiences of Aboriginal and Torres Strait Islander peoples under government policies, often referred to as "protection" or "assimilation" Acts, represent one of the darkest chapters in Australian history. These policies, introduced in the late 19th and early 20th centuries, profoundly altered the lives of Indigenous Australians. States and territories enacted their own versions of these laws, with Aboriginal Protection Boards enforcing the rules.

Key features of these policies included strict controls over movement, employment, marriage, and personal freedoms. Aboriginal people were confined to missions and reserves, often requiring permits to leave these spaces. The Acts allowed government-appointed protectors to manage wages, leading to financial exploitation. Families were torn apart under these laws, with many children forcibly removed from their homes to institutions or foster care, a practice that created the Stolen Generations.

The policies were justified under the guise of "protection," but they systematically disempowered Aboriginal communities, stripping them of autonomy and cultural identity. Forced assimilation sought to erase traditional practices, language, and connections to Country. The psychological toll of living under these restrictive and oppressive conditions created intergenerational trauma that persists today.

These Acts were not isolated events but part of a broader historical pattern of inequitable dealings with the government. Time and again, Aboriginal peoples engaged in good faith, only to find their concerns ignored or their rights undermined in favour of settler interests.

Cultural Survival Amidst Oppression

Despite the oppressive nature of these policies, Aboriginal communities demonstrated remarkable resilience and resistance. Cultural traditions, language, and ceremonies were often maintained in secret, defying government bans. Families found ways to preserve and pass down cultural knowledge, even in the face of relentless attempts to erase it.

This cultural survival was not without sacrifices. Many families deliberately concealed their Aboriginal identity to protect their children from being forcibly removed. Known as the "hidden generation," these individuals grew up disconnected from their heritage. Later in life, many embarked on complex journeys to rediscover their roots, reconnect with their communities, and reclaim their cultural identities.

Acts of resistance also emerged in the form of advocacy and political mobilisation. Aboriginal-run organisations fought for land rights, citizenship, and equality, laying the groundwork for landmark changes such as the 1967 Referendum and the *Native Title Act*. These efforts highlight the unyielding spirit of Aboriginal peoples in preserving their culture and fighting for their rights despite systemic attempts to suppress them.

Lessons from the Stolen Generations

The Stolen Generations epitomise the devastating human cost of the Acts. Under government policies, thousands of Aboriginal children were forcibly removed from their families and placed in institutions or foster care, often far from their communities. These children were denied access to their culture, language, and heritage, and many suffered abuse, neglect, and exploitation.

The trauma of the Stolen Generations reverberates across generations. For the children who were removed, the loss of identity and connection to their families often led to lifelong struggles with mental health, substance abuse, and a sense of displacement. For the families left behind, the pain of separation and the loss of cultural continuity remain a source of profound grief.

Addressing the legacy of the Stolen Generations is an essential part of Australia's reconciliation journey. Truth-telling initiatives, reparative actions, and programs that support cultural reconnection are critical to healing the wounds left by these policies. Efforts to revive endangered languages, preserve cultural practices, and strengthen community ties contribute to this ongoing process.

Living under the Acts was a period of profound hardship for Aboriginal peoples, marked by loss, trauma, and systemic disempowerment. Yet it was also a time of resilience and defiance, as communities found ways to survive, resist, and preserve their cultures.

Understanding this history is essential for fostering genuine reconciliation and respectful engagement. It reminds us of the resilience of Aboriginal peoples and the importance of empowering communities to lead their own paths toward healing and self-determination. The lessons of this era underscore the need for truth, equity, and inclusivity in all future engagements with Indigenous Australians.

6

The Hidden Generation

Concealing Identity for Survival

In the shadows of Australia's colonial history lies a less-discussed phenomenon—the emergence of the "hidden generation." These individuals, often born into families that chose or were forced to conceal their Aboriginal heritage, grew up disconnected from their cultural roots. This concealment was a deliberate strategy, born out of necessity, to survive the pervasive racism, discrimination, and policies that marked much of Australia's history.

The policies of assimilation and forced removal, such as those resulting in the Stolen Generations, placed immense pressure on Aboriginal families to hide their identity. Declaring oneself as Aboriginal often meant exposure to discrimination, loss of employment opportunities, and the looming threat of family separation. In response, families adopted strategies of cultural survival, opting to protect their children from the dangers of systemic racism by distancing them from their heritage.

Children of the hidden generation grew up without knowledge of their Indigenous roots, their cultural identity shielded by their parents' silence. This disconnection, while protective, carried profound consequences, leaving many individuals feeling alienated from their heritage and communities later in life.

Rediscovering Culture and Heritage

For members of the hidden generation, rediscovering their Aboriginal heritage is often a deeply personal and transformative journey. Many first learn of their roots through family revelations, genealogical research, or community connections. This discovery is frequently accompanied by mixed emotions, empowerment and joy at reclaiming their identity, but also grief and anger over what was lost.

The process of reconnecting with culture often involves engaging with community events, participating in language revival programs, or attending cultural camps. For some, it may include learning about the laws, customs, and traditions of their ancestors, guided by Elders and knowledge keepers.

This journey, however, is not without challenges. Individuals may face questions about their authenticity or struggle to navigate spaces where they feel like outsiders within their own culture. Yet, the resilience displayed by these individuals underscores the enduring strength of Aboriginal identity.

Implications for Reconnection and Healing

The stories of the hidden generation hold critical lessons for reconciliation and healing. Reconnection with culture is not just a personal journey; it is a collective process that strengthens the fabric of Aboriginal communities. Supporting this process requires providing spaces for cultural learning and healing, such as:

- **Language Revitalisation Programs:** Reviving Indigenous languages connects individuals to their heritage and strengthens cultural continuity.
- **Cultural Camps:** Offering immersive experiences in traditional practices helps bridge the gap between past and present.
- **Community Networks:** Creating spaces for shared stories and collective healing fosters a sense of belonging and mutual support.

Healing also necessitates broader societal change. Institutions must acknowledge the systemic forces that led to the emergence of the hidden generation and actively work to address ongoing inequities. Truth-telling initiatives, reparative actions, and inclusive policies are vital to creating an environment where no one feels the need to hide their identity.

The legacy of the hidden generation is a powerful reminder of the resilience of Aboriginal peoples and the importance of cultural connection. Their stories challenge us to reflect on the enduring impacts of colonisation and inspire us to build a future where every individual can celebrate their identity without fear or shame.

7

The Role of Elders, Leaders, and Knowledge Keepers

Traditional and Contemporary Roles

In Aboriginal societies, Elders, leaders, and knowledge keepers are the pillars of community structure and resilience, playing vital roles in preserving, guiding, and evolving their cultures. Each role carries distinct responsibilities, contributing uniquely to the strength and continuity of Aboriginal communities.

Historically, Elders were central figures, recognised for their wisdom, spiritual authority, and cultural knowledge. Their role was earned through years of learning, initiation, and community recognition. They upheld and transmitted laws, customs, and spiritual traditions, ensuring that cultural identity was preserved across generations. Elders were not only the custodians of knowledge but also moral guides and mediators within their communities.

In contemporary contexts, the role of Elders has evolved. While the ceremonial processes for recognition may have diminished in some areas, Elders remain the cornerstone of cultural guidance. They provide wisdom in navigating the challenges of modern governance while maintaining connections to traditional practices.

Leaders, historically tied to the role of Elders, often worked collaboratively within the community. Today, leadership has expanded to include managing programs, representing communities in political and legal arenas, and advocating for social, cultural, and environmental justice. Leaders often navigate complex systems and advocate for community needs in broader forums.

Knowledge keepers are specialists, dedicated to preserving specific aspects of Aboriginal culture, such as language, ecological practices, or ceremonial traditions. Their role is focused, often involving teaching younger generations and ensuring that unique cultural elements are not lost. Knowledge keepers might choose not to take on broader leadership or Elder roles, dedicating themselves instead to their specialised areas of expertise.

These roles, while interconnected, are distinct, and each contributes to the cultural and spiritual fabric of Aboriginal communities.

Navigating Self-Appointed Elders

One of the challenges in modern engagement is the emergence of self-appointed Elders who claim the title without their communities' endorsement. This phenomenon arises partly from the erosion of traditional recognition processes and the external pressure to engage with "Elders" in formal contexts.

Self-appointed Elders can dilute the authority of genuine Elders, provide inaccurate information or failing to uphold cultural responsibilities. They can create tensions within communities and lead to confusion for external organisations attempting to engage respectfully.

Engagement with Aboriginal communities requires due diligence. This includes verifying the legitimacy of those claiming to be Elders, seeking community endorsement, and consulting widely to ensure that the voices being elevated are authentic and representative.

Respecting Distinctions Between Roles

Understanding the distinctions between Elders, leaders, and knowledge keepers is essential for respectful engagement. While these roles often overlap, not all Elders are leaders, and not all leaders are knowledge keepers. Each role carries its unique responsibilities and strengths, and recognising these nuances ensures that engagement is inclusive and effective.

- **Elders** provide cultural and spiritual guidance, often serving as the moral compass of the community.
- **Leaders** advocate for community needs, represent their people in external forums, and manage programs or initiatives.

- **Knowledge keepers** specialise in preserving and teaching specific aspects of culture, such as language or ecological practices.

When engaging with Aboriginal communities, it is important to approach these roles with humility and respect. This involves seeking guidance from the community to identify the appropriate individuals to consult, respecting the protocols for recognising Elders, and ensuring that knowledge keepers and leaders are supported in their efforts to preserve and share cultural traditions. The roles of Elders, leaders, and knowledge keepers are the foundation of Aboriginal societies. While these roles have adapted to meet the challenges of modern times, they remain central to the preservation and resilience of Aboriginal cultures.

Respectful engagement begins with understanding and honouring these roles. By recognising their interconnected yet distinct contributions, we can build meaningful partnerships that support the cultural, social, and spiritual strength of Aboriginal communities. This understanding not only fosters trust and collaboration but also contributes to the broader goal of reconciliation and cultural revitalisation.

Ngullina

Ours; shared responsibility and custodianship

PART 2

BUILDING ENGAGEMENT PRACTICES

8

Recognising Red Flags

Effective engagement with Aboriginal and Torres Strait Islander communities requires vigilance against practices and behaviours that can undermine relationships and efforts. Recognising red flags — such as misrepresentation of authority, gatekeeping, and tokenism — ensures that engagement remains respectful, inclusive, and meaningful.

Misrepresentation of Authority

One of the most significant challenges in engagement is the misrepresentation of authority. This occurs when individuals or groups claim roles or responsibilities that they do not hold, often leading to confusion, mistrust, and misrepresentation of community voices.

In some cases, individuals might present themselves as Elders, leaders, or spokespersons without the endorsement or recognition of their community. These self-appointed figures can mislead external organisations, resulting in decisions or actions that do not align with the community's needs or cultural protocols.

Red flags include:

- A lack of visible support or acknowledgment from the community for the individual's claims.
- Discrepancies between what the individual advocates and the broader community's priorities.
- Claims of exclusive authority to speak or act on behalf of the community without proper consultation.

To address this issue, organisations must undertake due diligence. Consulting widely within the community, verifying claims of authority, and seeking guidance from recognised Traditional Owners, Elders, and community leaders can help ensure the right voices are involved in decision-making.

Gatekeeping and Undermining Other Groups

The term gatekeeping is often used with negative connotations, but in reality, it describes a common dynamic found across all sectors, not just in Aboriginal communities.

Gatekeepers are people who, through time, experience, and relationship-building, hold informal influence over who gets access to certain networks, spaces, or knowledge. They exist in communities, organisations, and institutions everywhere, and they are not inherently a problem.

In many Aboriginal communities, gatekeepers are Elders, long-standing community leaders, or staff from local organisations who have invested years—sometimes decades—building trust, responding to community needs, and holding things together during difficult times. Their role is often protective, not obstructive. Most of the time, gatekeepers simply want to be respected, included, and informed. When approached with transparency and respect, they are frequently generous, supportive, and instrumental in ensuring that engagement is meaningful and culturally safe.

It is neither appropriate nor respectful to demand access to a gatekeeper's personal or professional contact list. These networks have been built through lived experience, family ties, and years of commitment to the community. Expecting that access without trust or context ignores the time and responsibility it takes to maintain these relationships.

That said, gatekeeping can become problematic when it shifts from coordination to control. This happens when individuals or groups present themselves as the only legitimate voice or point of contact for a community, intentionally or unintentionally excluding others. In some cases, it may escalate into actively undermining other Aboriginal organisations or individuals. This behaviour can disrupt engagement and sow division, leading to unbalanced outcomes that may be harmful.

Problematic gatekeeping may include:

- Dismissing the legitimacy of other groups or leaders.
- Controlling access to meetings, resources, or information to limit participation.

- Discouraging collaboration or fostering competition between community members or organisations.

These behaviours are usually rooted in deeper dynamics, such as historical grievances, mistrust of government processes, or fears that poor engagement will leave lasting damage. Many gatekeepers have seen programs come and go, with little benefit left behind. Their caution is often warranted.

To ensure respectful and inclusive engagement, organisations should:

- Recognise the value that long-term community leaders and gatekeepers bring.
- Engage with multiple stakeholders to ensure a broad and representative range of voices are heard.
- Avoid assuming that one person or group can speak on behalf of an entire community.
- Be transparent about intentions, processes, and outcomes.
- Allow time for trust to develop, and don't rush past important relationships.

Gatekeepers are not the enemy of engagement; they are often its backbone. But, as with all roles, their influence must be balanced with inclusivity, transparency, and respect for the full spectrum of voices within a community. When acknowledged and supported appropriately, gatekeepers can help facilitate an informed, respectful, and locally grounded engagement. Ignoring them or misjudging their intent can create tension and risk long-term consequences far beyond the life of a project.

Relational Authority, Contact Lists, and Continuity of Engagement

In Aboriginal engagement work, contact lists are often treated as a practical tool, handed over during staff transitions or stored for future access. These lists usually represent something much deeper: years of cultural obligation, kinship ties, community trust, and lived experience. Relationships are not simply "work contacts" in a conventional sense. They are built through story, ceremony, shared history, and accountability.

I experienced this firsthand while working in a short-term role at the City of Gold Coast. As my contract neared its end, my line leader asked me to hand over my full contact list to the organisation. On the surface, this may have appeared routine, but it was deeply inappropriate.

The contact list I held was not built during my contract. I brought those relationships with me into the role. Many of the people on that list were my relatives, cultural leaders, or individuals who trusted me because of who I am, not because of my job title. To hand over those details would have been a breach of that trust and a serious cultural overstep. It would have treated relational authority as an asset owned by the institution, rather than a responsibility carried by the individual. That expectation ignored the foundational principle that trust in community engagement is earned, not inherited.

In contrast, in my current role, I'm working intentionally with the team to build a contact list that supports ongoing engagement. This is a short-term contract, too, but the approach is very different and much more appropriate.

Rather than simply transferring names and numbers, I focus on introducing the team, providing context, and supporting relationship-building. I help them understand not just who to speak to, but how, when, and why. I encourage the team to take their time, to ask respectfully, and to understand local dynamics before engaging. In doing so, we are setting up a shared system that will outlast my time in the role and support continuity of respectful engagement.

This difference matters. It highlights an important principle: while information can be shared, trust cannot. Relationships built through culture, kinship, and community cannot be "handed over" like a spreadsheet. Expecting this is not only ineffective, it risks damaging community trust and undermining the very engagement efforts an organisation seeks to sustain.

For organisations and leaders in Aboriginal engagement work, the lesson is clear:

- Do not assume that relationships built by Aboriginal staff are transferable assets.
- Do not demand personal networks without understanding how they were formed.
- Instead, support staff to facilitate introductions and provide guidance for respectful engagement that continues well beyond a contract's end.

Ethical engagement is not just about who you know; it's about how you hold that knowledge and whether you use it with respect.

Avoiding Tokenism in Engagement Efforts

Tokenism occurs when Aboriginal people are included in engagement efforts superficially, often as a symbolic gesture rather than as meaningful contributors. Tokenism can undermine trust, erode credibility, and perpetuate the systemic exclusion of Aboriginal voices.

Indicators of tokenism include:

- Engaging with Aboriginal representatives only to meet funding or compliance requirements.
- Limiting Aboriginal involvement to ceremonial or symbolic roles without real decision-making power.
- Relying on a single Aboriginal voice to represent an entire community or multiple groups.

To avoid tokenism, organisations must:

- Commit to genuine partnerships that prioritise Aboriginal leadership and input at all stages of a project.
- Engage multiple voices from within the community to reflect its diversity.
- Ensure that Aboriginal participants are empowered to contribute meaningfully and equitably to decision-making processes.

By moving beyond tokenistic practices, organisations can build relationships based on mutual respect, trust, and shared purpose.

What This Means in Practice

Recognising red flags such as misrepresentation of authority, gatekeeping, and tokenism is critical to fostering respectful and effective engagement with Aboriginal communities. Addressing these challenges requires diligence, transparency, and a commitment to inclusivity.

By actively identifying and addressing these issues, organisations can ensure that their engagement efforts are authentic, representative, and aligned with the needs and aspirations of the communities they seek to serve. This approach builds the trust and collaboration necessary for meaningful partnerships and long-term success.

yarga

wind

9

Engagement Is Not Salesmanship

Recognising the Ethical Boundaries of Influence

In recent years, I was invited to interview for an engagement position on a large, federally funded infrastructure project. This capital works initiative spanned multiple states and directly affected land, including Crown land, which required Traditional Owner consultation and engagement.

The interview progressed well until a moment of subtle but revealing tension. The human resources team, which was conducting the interview, asked a question that raised a red flag. Though veiled in language, it was clear that what they really wanted to know was whether I would be capable of persuading, or perhaps more bluntly, selling, the project to Traditional Owners.

I paused, then responded with a question of my own: "Are you looking for a salesman or an engagement officer?"

That moment landed poorly. From that point, it became evident that I would not be progressing further in the process.

Reflecting on this experience highlights a crucial misunderstanding that continues to undermine Indigenous engagement across sectors. Engagement is not about persuasion. It is not about leading someone to a predetermined What This Means in Practice or seeking to secure their agreement at all costs. Engagement is about respect, truth, and transparency.

When Traditional Owners are approached in good faith, it must be with the understanding that their answer, whatever it may be, is valid. Engagement is not a performance nor a transaction. It is a process rooted in listening, mutual understanding, and the recognition of rights. To reduce it to a marketing exercise is to ignore the very principles that guide ethical practice in this field.

This chapter serves as a reminder that genuine engagement does not begin with a pitch; it starts with humility. Practitioners must recognise that they are entering into a relationship with communities that hold their own governance, authority, and decision-making processes. When engagement is used to manipulate or coerce, it erodes trust, damages relationships, and can cause long-term harm to community-government relations.

Those tasked with engagement roles must be empowered to facilitate dialogue, not to close deals. Suppose the success of a project is measured by whether Traditional Owners agree with it. In that case, organisations must first ask whether the project genuinely considers their concerns, values, and rights.

Engagement officers are not salespeople. They are bridges, between governments and communities, between policy and people. But those bridges must be built on foundations of respect and truth, not persuasion and performance.

10

Cultural Protocols: Beyond the Catchphrase

Defining Cultural Protocols

Cultural protocols are the established and accepted ways of interacting with and showing respect to Aboriginal peoples, their culture, traditions, and Country. These protocols encompass values, customs, and beliefs that dictate appropriate behaviour within Aboriginal communities. They are not mere formalities but are deeply embedded in spiritual, cultural, and historical contexts.

For example, respect for Elders as custodians of knowledge is a fundamental protocol. Elders are often sought for their guidance, wisdom, and approval on matters affecting the community. Another key protocol is the Acknowledgement of Country, a practice of recognising the Traditional Owners of the land and their enduring connection to it. Obtaining permission before using cultural knowledge, stories, or resources is another integral aspect that reflects the importance of consent and collaboration. Cultural protocols vary from one region and community to another, highlighting the diversity within Aboriginal cultures. Navigating these differences requires a commitment to understanding, adaptability, and respectful engagement.

Implementing Protocols with Integrity

The use of cultural protocols can often risk becoming a hollow exercise if not implemented with genuine commitment and understanding. Phrases like "cultural protocols" must transcend tokenistic acknowledgment and become the foundation for meaningful practices.

Implementing cultural protocols effectively begins with thorough research and preparation. This involves understanding the unique history, traditions, and specific expectations of the community involved. Guidance from Elders, cultural advisors, or other Aboriginal representatives ensures that practices remain authentic and culturally appropriate.

Active engagement is a crucial component. Genuine collaboration requires respectful dialogue, open-mindedness, and a willingness to listen. Organisations and individuals must approach these interactions without preconceived assumptions or rigid agendas. Cultural protocols should also be embedded into organisational policies and processes, ensuring they are consistently upheld rather than treated as one-off gestures.

Regular review and adaptation of engagement strategies help maintain alignment with community needs. Feedback from community members can provide insights into areas for improvement, ensuring that protocols remain relevant and impactful.

Avoiding Superficial Engagement

Superficial acknowledgment of cultural protocols can erode trust and damage relationships with Aboriginal communities. For instance, using cultural practices merely to meet compliance requirements or to project inclusivity, without genuine collaboration, reflects tokenism. Similarly, failing to understand or accurately convey the significance of these protocols misrepresents their value and undermines their purpose.

Superficial efforts are often perceived as insincere, which can alienate communities and hinder future engagement. To counter this, organisations must focus on building meaningful relationships based on mutual respect and understanding. A genuine commitment to respecting and implementing cultural protocols is essential to fostering trust and collaboration.

Cultural protocols are far more than symbolic gestures; they are the cornerstone of respectful and effective engagement with Aboriginal communities. By approaching these protocols with sincerity and a commitment to understanding, individuals and organisations can preserve cultural integrity and build lasting, mutually beneficial relationships.

Authentic engagement with cultural protocols ensures that they serve as meaningful pathways to inclusion and respect. In doing so, we honour the depth and diversity of Aboriginal cultures while contributing to reconciliation and stronger partnerships.

Business, Men's Business, Women's Business, and Sorry Business

Business in Aboriginal Communities

In Aboriginal culture, "business" refers to more than economic or transactional activities; it encompasses a range of ceremonial, cultural, and communal practices integral to maintaining social cohesion and connection to Country. Business is deeply rooted in tradition and is often carried out in specific places that hold cultural significance, such as Bora Rings.

Bora Rings serve as a powerful example of how Aboriginal business was, and continues to be, organised. These circular earthen structures, often arranged in clusters, are found throughout Aboriginal lands and were historically used for various purposes: communal gatherings, Men's Business, and Women's Business.

Bora Rings and Men's Business

In many communities, certain Bora Rings were designated exclusively for Men's Business. These spaces were sacred, serving as sites for ceremonies, initiations, and governance. Men gathered here to perform rituals that strengthened their connection to ancestors, Country, and law.

Men's Business often involved the passing of knowledge that was restricted to men, such as skills for hunting, lore, and spiritual practices. Access to these Bora Rings was strictly controlled, with cultural protocols ensuring that only initiated men could participate or enter.

When engaging with Aboriginal communities today, respecting the boundaries of Men's Business remains essential. Discussions about traditional governance or land management, for example, may require the involvement of male Elders or Traditional Owners who hold this specific cultural knowledge.

Bora Rings and Women's Business

Similarly, certain Bora Rings were reserved for Women's Business. These sacred spaces were used for ceremonies related to fertility, caregiving, and the nurturing aspects of community life. Women gathered here to celebrate life cycles, pass on cultural knowledge, and conduct ceremonies that upheld their roles as caretakers of family and Country.

The importance of Women's Business highlights the distinct roles and responsibilities of women in Aboriginal culture. Just as with Men's Business, respecting the protocols surrounding Women's Business is critical for meaningful engagement. This may involve holding gender-specific consultations or ensuring that culturally sensitive topics are discussed only with appropriate female representatives.

Bora Rings and Communal Business

Not all Bora Rings were gender specific. Some were designed for communal gatherings, where the entire community would come together to perform ceremonies, resolve disputes, or celebrate important events. These communal Bora Rings symbolised unity, reinforcing the community's interconnectedness and shared responsibilities to one another and to the land.

When engaging with Aboriginal communities today, understanding the concept of communal business is important for fostering inclusivity. Communal gatherings often serve as spaces for collective decision-making, storytelling, and cultural expression.

Sorry Business

Sorry Business, while not directly connected to Bora Rings, is another vital aspect of Aboriginal cultural practices. This refers to the rituals and ceremonies associated with mourning and grief. Just as Bora Rings were respected as sacred spaces, the periods of mourning during Sorry Business must also be respected as sacred times.

Engagement efforts may need to pause during Sorry Business to allow the community to grieve and honour their loved ones. Ignoring these cultural obligations can lead to mistrust or harm relationships.

Practical Implications for Engagement

Using Bora Rings as a framework, the principles of Aboriginal business, whether communal, Men's, or Women's, provide a guide for respectful engagement:

- **Cultural Sensitivity:** Recognise the significance of spaces and practices tied to Men's, Women's, or communal business, and respect their boundaries.

- **Gender-Specific Engagement:** When topics align with Men's or Women's Business, ensure consultations are gender-appropriate and led by individuals who hold cultural authority.
- **Inclusion and Unity:** For communal matters, create spaces where all voices can be heard while respecting the collective decision-making process.
- **Flexibility During Sorry Business:** Be prepared to pause engagement activities and adapt timelines to honour periods of mourning.

The use of Bora Rings for Men's, Women's, and communal gatherings illustrates the structured and deeply respectful way Aboriginal communities approach cultural business. These spaces and practices reflect the importance of understanding roles, responsibilities, and protocols when engaging with Aboriginal people.

By respecting the distinctions between Men's Business, Women's Business, communal gatherings, and Sorry Business, organisations and individuals can foster relationships built on trust and cultural understanding. Engagement is not just about communication—it is about recognising and honouring the cultural foundations that continue to guide Aboriginal communities today.

11

Identifying Stakeholders

Mapping Community Dynamics

Identifying stakeholders within Aboriginal and Torres Strait Islander communities begins with understanding the dynamics that shape their structures and relationships. Communities are rarely homogenous, often comprising diverse groups with distinct roles, responsibilities, and perspectives. These dynamics are influenced by factors such as historical context, cultural practices, and geographical connections to Country.

Effective stakeholder identification requires careful mapping of these dynamics. It involves recognising the key groups, organisations, and individuals who hold cultural authority, influence decision-making, or represent specific interests within the community. This process includes understanding traditional leadership roles, such as Elders and Traditional Owners, as well as contemporary structures, such as Aboriginal-run organisations, community councils, and youth groups.

Mapping community dynamics helps ensure that engagement efforts are inclusive and comprehensive. It avoids the pitfalls of relying solely on a single individual or group, ensuring that diverse voices are heard and respected.

Understanding the Diverse Roles of Stakeholders

Stakeholders in Aboriginal communities serve a wide range of roles, each contributing uniquely to the community's governance, culture, and development. These roles include but are not limited to Elders, leaders, knowledge keepers, Traditional Owners, cultural advisors, and representatives of Aboriginal organisations.

Elders are often the custodians of cultural knowledge and traditions, providing guidance and wisdom. Leaders may take on advocacy roles, representing their communities in negotiations with external parties. Knowledge keepers focus on preserving specific aspects of culture, such as language, ceremonies, or ecological practices. Traditional Owners maintain responsibilities tied to their specific Country, acting as stewards of land and heritage.

Organisations such as land councils, health services, and educational bodies also play critical roles in advancing community interests. Each of these stakeholders brings unique insights and expertise, highlighting the importance of engaging with a broad spectrum of voices.

Recognising these diverse roles ensures that engagement efforts are culturally appropriate and contextually relevant. It also helps to identify potential overlaps or gaps in representation, fostering more effective collaboration.

Ensuring Equitable Representation

Equitable representation is a cornerstone of respectful and inclusive engagement. It involves ensuring that all relevant voices within a community can contribute to discussions, decisions, and initiatives. This requires proactive efforts to include groups that may be underrepresented or marginalised, such as women, youth, or those disconnected from their Country due to displacement.

Equitable representation also means balancing traditional and contemporary perspectives. While Elders and Traditional Owners often hold cultural authority, younger generations bring valuable insights into contemporary challenges and opportunities. Engagement efforts should aim to create spaces where all voices are valued and heard.

To achieve equitable representation, it is important to:

- Conduct broad consultations to identify all relevant stakeholders.
- Create inclusive forums that encourage participation from diverse groups.
- Ensure that engagement processes are transparent and accessible, addressing potential barriers to involvement.

By fostering equitable representation, organisations can build stronger, more inclusive partnerships that reflect the full diversity of Aboriginal communities.

What This Means in Practice

Identifying stakeholders is a foundational step in effective engagement with Aboriginal communities. By mapping community dynamics, understanding the diverse roles of stakeholders, and ensuring equitable representation, organisations can create inclusive, respectful, and impactful partnerships.

This approach not only strengthens relationships but also ensures that engagement efforts reflect the community's complexity and diversity. By prioritising these foundational practices, organisations can create meaningful partnerships and achieve shared goals while respecting and celebrating Aboriginal cultures and perspectives.

giwa

goanna

12

Building Blocks of Engagement

Teamwork, Communication, and Time Management

Successful engagement with Aboriginal and Torres Strait Islander communities depends on strong teamwork, clear communication, and effective time management. These elements form the foundation of any collaborative effort, ensuring that all participants work towards shared goals cohesively and respectfully.

Teamwork involves recognising the strengths and expertise of everyone involved, both within the community and the external organisations engaging with them. This requires fostering an environment of mutual respect and trust in which every team member's voice is valued. Teams must also include cultural advisors or representatives who can provide insights into community expectations, cultural protocols, and local dynamics.

Clear communication is another essential component. It involves more than just exchanging information; it requires active listening, cultural sensitivity, and the ability to convey ideas that resonate with all stakeholders. Effective communication also includes acknowledging language differences and adapting messages to ensure inclusivity and understanding.

Time management is particularly important when working with Aboriginal communities, as engagement often unfolds at a pace dictated by cultural and community priorities. Flexibility is key, as rigid timelines can conflict with the slower, relationship-focused processes valued in many communities. Respecting this tempo while balancing organisational needs is a vital skill for any engagement team.

Planning for Inclusive Schedules

Inclusivity in scheduling means ensuring that all stakeholders have the opportunity to participate in engagement activities. This involves considering the unique needs and circumstances of different groups within the community, such as Elders, youth, and those with work or family commitments.

When planning schedules, it is important to consult with community members to identify times and locations that are convenient and accessible. For example, daytime meetings may not suit working participants, while remote or outdoor locations may present challenges for some Elders or community members with mobility issues.

Engagement schedules should also align with cultural practices and seasonal events. For example, certain times of the year may be significant for cultural ceremonies or activities, and these should be respected in planning processes. Additionally, allowing for flexibility in meeting times can accommodate unforeseen delays or changes in community availability.

An inclusive schedule demonstrates respect for the community's priorities and fosters greater participation. It also helps to build trust, as stakeholders feel their time and commitments are being valued.

Tools for Productive Engagement

Utilising the right tools and strategies can significantly enhance the effectiveness of engagement efforts. These tools can include:

- **Facilitation Techniques:** Structured discussions, breakout groups, or storytelling sessions encourage active participation and ensure all voices are heard.
- **Visual Aids and Resources:** Maps, diagrams, and culturally relevant materials can help clarify complex information and make engagement more interactive.
- **Technology:** Tools such as video conferencing or digital surveys can increase accessibility, particularly for communities in remote locations, while ensuring participants who cannot attend in person can still contribute.

- **Feedback Mechanisms:** Providing avenues for community members to share their thoughts and concerns, such as anonymous surveys or suggestion boxes, promotes transparency and inclusivity.

Selecting culturally appropriate tools tailored to the specific community is critical. Engagement efforts should avoid imposing external systems that do not resonate with the community's values or ways of working.

What This Means in Practice

The building blocks of engagement—teamwork, communication, and time management—are the foundation of respectful and effective collaboration. By planning inclusive schedules and leveraging the right tools, organisations can foster environments that encourage participation, build trust, and support productive dialogue.

These elements ensure that engagement is not only effective but also reflective of the communities' needs and aspirations. By prioritising these foundational practices, organisations can create meaningful partnerships and achieve shared goals while respecting and celebrating Aboriginal cultures and perspectives.

13

Engagement Etiquette

Active Listening

Listening to What is Said—and What is Not Said

Active listening is more than simply hearing words. It is a conscious, respectful, and deliberate effort to fully understand what is being communicated, both verbally and non-verbally. Within Aboriginal communities, where knowledge is often shared through story, silence, and gesture, the ability to listen with intention is critical. It can mean the difference between a respectful engagement and a failed relationship.

Active listening involves giving your full attention to the speaker, suspending judgement, and allowing them to speak without interruption. It requires an awareness that meaning is often layered; what is not said can be just as important as what is spoken. A pause, a look, or the choice to remain silent might hold deep cultural significance. In some cases, it may signal caution, discomfort, or disagreement—though this may not be explicitly stated.

To practise **active listening** in an Indigenous engagement setting:

- **Be Present:** Put away distractions, make eye contact if culturally appropriate, and bring your focus entirely to the person or people speaking.
- **Use Cues Thoughtfully:** Nods, facial expressions, and short verbal acknowledgements can show that you are engaged but be careful not to interrupt.
- Phrases like "yes" or "I understand" can help show you are engaged, but do not overdo them. Sometimes, listening quietly without interrupting is the most respectful response.
- **Do Not Rush to Fill Silence**: Silence is not a void; it often holds meaning. Be patient. A speaker may be thinking, waiting for the right words, or testing whether you are worthy of hearing more.
- **Reflect and Clarify**: When appropriate, gently repeat or summarise what was said to check your understanding, without putting words in their mouth.
- **Avoid Assumptions**: Let go of your own frameworks or expectations. Listen for the speaker's meaning, not just for facts or outcomes.
- **Show Respect for Context**: Some topics are not meant

to be unpacked in one sitting. Active listening includes accepting that further explanation may come in time, or not at all.

When engagement is rooted in active listening, trust is built, and a more honest, culturally safe space is created. Listening is not passive; it is one of the most powerful tools in any respectful engagement process.

Practising Diplomacy and Due Diligence

Engagement requires navigating complex dynamics with sensitivity and diplomacy. Communities may have diverse or conflicting views, and it is crucial to approach these situations with tact and impartiality. Diplomacy involves acknowledging all perspectives without favouritism, ensuring that engagement remains inclusive and fair.

Due diligence complements diplomacy by ensuring that efforts are well-researched, thorough, and aligned with cultural protocols. This includes:

- Understanding the community's history and social dynamics before initiating engagement.
- Consulting widely to ensure all relevant voices are included.
- Verifying the legitimacy of individuals claiming authority to speak or act on behalf of the community.

Practising diplomacy and due diligence builds credibility and demonstrates a commitment to respectful and meaningful engagement. It also helps to mitigate potential conflicts or misunderstandings, creating a smoother path toward collaboration.

Follow-Up as a Key to Success

Follow-up is an often-overlooked yet essential component of effective engagement. It reflects respect for the community's contributions and ensures that discussions translate into actionable outcomes.

Following up involves maintaining open communication after initial meetings or consultations. This includes:

- Providing updates on the progress of agreed actions or initiatives.
- Sharing feedback on how community input has been incorporated.
- Continuing to seek input and address any concerns that may arise.

Consistency in follow-up demonstrates accountability and builds trust. It assures the community that their voices are valued and that their contributions are driving meaningful change.

Failure to follow up, on the other hand, can lead to frustration, disappointment, and erosion of trust. Communities may feel disregarded or tokenised if their input does not result in tangible outcomes or ongoing dialogue.

What This Means in Practice

Engagement etiquette is not just about following protocols; it is about embodying respect, sensitivity, and accountability throughout the engagement process. By listening attentively, practising diplomacy and due diligence, and prioritising follow-up, organisations can foster trust and build stronger relationships with Aboriginal and Torres Strait Islander communities.

These practices ensure that engagement is not a one-off exercise but a sustained, meaningful partnership. By valuing the community's voices and perspectives, organisations can create pathways to collaboration that are both respectful and impactful.

Kaialgumm

Authority / rightful power

PART 3

CULTIVATING RESPECTFUL RELATIONSHIPS

charara

track

14

The Importance of Cultural Competency

Understanding History, Culture, and Language

Cultural competency begins with a foundational understanding of the history, culture, and language of Aboriginal and Torres Strait Islander peoples. The history of colonisation, dispossession, and systemic discrimination has profoundly shaped the lives and communities of Indigenous Australians. Recognising this context is essential to engaging respectfully and effectively.

Culture and language are central to identity and connection to Country. Aboriginal peoples' spiritual and cultural practices are deeply tied to the land, and their languages reflect unique ways of understanding and interacting with the world. The disruption caused by colonisation has led to the loss or endangerment of many traditional languages and practices.

Engagement efforts must respect and honour these histories and cultural practices. Demonstrating knowledge of and sensitivity to these elements shows respect, fosters trust, and ensures that engagement aligns with community values.

Addressing Cultural Overloading and Community Demands

Aboriginal communities often face disproportionate demands on their time and resources due to repeated engagement efforts by governments, organisations, and other stakeholders. This phenomenon, known as cultural overloading, places a significant strain on communities, particularly on Elders and cultural leaders who are already balancing numerous responsibilities.

If external organisations and individuals are paid for their engagement efforts, it is only fair that Aboriginal community members are also compensated for their time, knowledge, and contributions. Their cultural expertise is invaluable, and recognising this through fair compensation reflects respect and equity.

Fair compensation often takes the form of sitting fees. Sitting fees acknowledge the time and cultural expertise of Aboriginal participants in consultations, decision-making processes, and cultural guidance. This compensation is essential to ensuring equity and to demonstrate the value of Aboriginal contributions.

Moving Beyond Performative Actions

Cultural competency requires moving beyond symbolic or performative actions that lack genuine substance. While acknowledgments of Country and similar practices are important, they are insufficient if not accompanied by meaningful efforts to support Aboriginal communities.

Performative actions might include token consultations, superficial partnerships, or activities focused solely on compliance. These practices risk alienating communities and undermining trust.

True cultural competency involves embedding cultural awareness into all aspects of organisational practices. This includes fostering genuine partnerships, prioritising Aboriginal leadership in decision-making, and ensuring that actions are guided by the community's needs and aspirations rather than external agendas. Meaningful engagement reflects a commitment to shared outcomes and mutual respect.

What This Means in Practice

Cultural competency is essential to respectful and effective engagement. By understanding the history, culture, and language of Aboriginal and Torres Strait Islander peoples, addressing cultural overloading, and ensuring fair compensation through sitting fees, organisations can demonstrate a sincere commitment to equitable relationships.

This approach moves beyond superficial gestures, fostering meaningful collaboration and mutual growth. By embracing cultural competency, organisations can build trust, respect, and successful partnerships with Aboriginal communities, contributing to broader reconciliation efforts.

15

Avoiding Acronyms and Initials

The Case for Clear and Inclusive Communication

Effective communication is fundamental to meaningful engagement. In working with Aboriginal and Torres Strait Islander communities, avoiding acronyms and initials is crucial to ensuring clarity and inclusivity. While acronyms are common in government and corporate communications, they can create unnecessary barriers to understanding and exclude those unfamiliar with institutional jargon.

For example, referring to the Kombumerri Aboriginal Corporation for Culture by its full name rather than an acronym (e.g., KACC) demonstrates respect for the organisation's cultural identity. It also ensures that the meaning and significance of the name are preserved, fostering a sense of transparency and inclusivity in dialogue.

Clear communication ensures that all participants, regardless of their background, can engage on equal footing. This approach avoids alienating community members and builds stronger relationships by valuing their involvement and insights.

Promoting Respect Through Language

Language is a cornerstone of Aboriginal culture, serving as a medium for storytelling, oral traditions, and the preservation of heritage. By avoiding acronyms and initials, organisations align their communication practices with these cultural values. Using complete names and terms fosters respect for language as a core component of cultural identity.

Acronyms can also create a sense of exclusivity, inadvertently marginalising those unfamiliar with the terms. This undermines trust and inclusivity, key elements of successful engagement. In a context where mutual understanding is paramount, taking the time to use full names and clear language demonstrates a genuine commitment to fostering equitable communication.

Practical Applications in Documentation and Dialogue

Avoiding acronyms and initials does not compromise efficiency; rather, it enhances comprehension and respect. Practical steps for applying this principle include:

- **Introducing Full Terms First:** When referring to an organisation or program, always use its full name initially. If abbreviations are necessary, introduce them only after the full term has been explained.

- **Adapting to the Audience:** Tailor communication to the participants, prioritising clarity and formality in Indigenous engagements.
- **Encouraging Questions:** Create an environment where participants feel comfortable seeking clarification, reinforcing open dialogue and mutual understanding.
- **Leading by Example:** Demonstrate the importance of using full terms in speech and writing to encourage others to follow suit.

Transparency and inclusivity are also critical in written documentation. When preparing materials such as meeting agendas, reports, or presentations, ensure that full names and explanations are provided for any unfamiliar terms. This practice avoids assumptions about prior knowledge and ensures that all stakeholders feel included and respected.

What This Means in Practice

Avoiding acronyms and initials in Indigenous engagements is more than a stylistic choice; it is a meaningful act of respect and cultural awareness. By prioritising clear and inclusive communication, organisations honour the values and traditions of the communities they engage with.

This practice strengthens relationships, fosters trust, and ensures that communication is both effective and impactful. By taking this seemingly small but significant step, organisations contribute to a broader culture of respect and inclusivity in their engagement efforts.

Wunnalei Woba Kulgoll

Stop / caution; pause before action

16

Creating a Safe Space

Strategies for Inclusive and Respectful Dialogue

Creating a safe space for dialogue is essential to building trust and fostering meaningful engagement with Aboriginal communities. A safe space is not merely a physical setting but an environment where all participants — Aboriginal stakeholders, facilitators, and other contributors — feel respected, valued, and empowered to express themselves without fear of judgment, marginalisation, or harm.

Engagement practices must go beyond superficial efforts like informal gatherings or tokenistic gestures. The days of assuming that a "sausage sizzle" is sufficient to address community concerns are long over. Such approaches can trivialise the significance of the engagement and risk alienating participants. Instead, engagement must be carefully tailored to the community's cultural and social dynamics, while ensuring the process supports mutual respect and understanding for everyone involved.

A key element of inclusive dialogue is recognising the diversity within Aboriginal communities. Just as it would be inappropriate to place opposing political parties like the LNP and Labor in the same room and expect consensus, the same principle applies to Aboriginal organisations. Communities often have distinct histories, priorities, and even conflicting viewpoints. Forcing everyone into a single forum risks exacerbating tensions and undermining the effectiveness of the engagement.

Preparing for Multiple Engagement Sessions

To respect the diversity of perspectives and ensure productive engagement, organisations should be prepared to conduct multiple sessions to accommodate relevant stakeholders. This approach provides the flexibility to address unique needs and dynamics within the community while fostering a safe space for all participants.

Before scheduling sessions, it is important to consult with participants to gauge their comfort with the proposed attendee list. Asking stakeholders whether they feel comfortable with the people invited helps proactively address potential conflicts or tensions. If participants express discomfort or concerns, it is crucial to accommodate them by organising separate sessions tailored to their needs.

Separate consultations may also benefit facilitators and other contributors, providing them with an environment where they feel safe and supported in fulfilling their roles. Facilitators must be empowered to maintain neutrality and guide discussions without fear of backlash or bias, ensuring the dialogue remains productive and respectful for everyone involved.

A Two-Way Street

Creating a safe space is a two-way street. It must extend beyond the Aboriginal community to include facilitators, organisational representatives, and other contributors. Everyone involved in the engagement process should feel secure in expressing their views, asking questions, and participating without fear of hostility or harm.

Facilitators often navigate complex dynamics and maintain balance in discussions. They must feel supported by their organisations and confident that their neutrality will be respected. Clear guidelines, training, and debriefing sessions can help facilitators manage their roles effectively while feeling safe in their environment.

Participants also play a role in fostering this mutual safety by adhering to agreed-upon norms of respectful communication, active listening, and collaboration. Clear expectations set at the outset of engagement sessions help ensure a constructive, inclusive environment.

Engagement requires mutual effort. Both the Aboriginal stakeholders and the organisations initiating engagement must prioritise respect, understanding, and accountability to create an environment where everyone's safety and well-being are upheld.

Transparency with All Parties

Transparency is essential for building trust and fostering mutual respect. Participants must clearly understand the purpose of the engagement, who else is being consulted, and how their input will be used. Being open about who is involved and what the process entails reassures all parties that the engagement is fair and inclusive.

Organisations can build this transparency by openly communicating with all participants about:

- The goals and scope of the engagement process.
- The roles and identities of other stakeholders being consulted.

How input will be incorporated into outcomes and decisions. Transparency fosters trust not only between organisations and Aboriginal communities but also among the diverse participants involved in the engagement process.

Managing Group Dynamics in Engagement Sessions

Group dynamics can significantly impact the success of engagement efforts. Aboriginal communities, like any group, include a wide range of relationships, alliances, and differences. These dynamics must be managed with sensitivity and respect to create an environment conducive to productive dialogue.

Facilitators must remain impartial and ensure that all participants feel heard and respected. A skilled facilitator recognises when to intervene to prevent dominant voices from overshadowing others and ensures everyone can contribute meaningfully.

Creating a safe space for engagement is about fostering respect, understanding, and security for everyone involved. It requires acknowledging the diverse perspectives within Aboriginal communities and ensuring that facilitators and organisational representatives also feel supported and valued in their roles.

By tailoring engagement to specific needs, preparing for multiple sessions when necessary, ensuring transparency with all parties, and recognising that engagement is a two-way street, organisations can create an inclusive and productive environment. A safe space is not just about physical comfort or cultural awareness; it is about mutual respect and shared responsibility, laying the groundwork for meaningful collaboration and lasting partnerships.

17

Cultural Awareness Training

Designing Effective Programs

Cultural awareness training is a cornerstone for fostering understanding and respect between organisations and Aboriginal communities. However, designing effective programs requires more than surface-level content or one-off sessions. Programs must delve deeply into history, address unconscious biases, and equip participants with practical skills for meaningful engagement. Key elements of effective training include:

- **Facilitation by Aboriginal Experts:** Training should be led or co-designed by Aboriginal facilitators who bring cultural knowledge and lived experience.
- **Local Relevance:** Content must reflect the specific history, traditions, and protocols of the Aboriginal community being engaged. This ensures the training is meaningful and applicable.

- **Interactive Learning:** Engaging participants through activities like case studies, role-playing, and discussions fosters deeper understanding and retention.
- **Ongoing Commitment:** Cultural awareness training should not be treated as a one-off event. Regular follow-up sessions and continuous learning opportunities create lasting change.
- **Actionable Outcomes:** Participants should leave the training with clear strategies for applying their learning to their roles and interactions.
- **Supporting Engagement Efforts:** The training should equip participants with the skills to identify who to engage, understand their histories, and respect their cultural practices. This ensures that future interactions are well-informed and culturally appropriate.

Programs that incorporate these elements inspire genuine change within organisations, fostering respect and effective collaboration with Aboriginal communities.

Overcoming Challenges and Resistance

Despite its importance, cultural awareness training often encounters resistance or challenges that undermine its effectiveness. Common issues include superficial content, tokenistic approaches, and participant resistance.

To address these challenges:

- **Combat Superficiality:** Avoid generic cultural facts and instead focus on the systemic issues and power dynamics that shape Aboriginal experiences.
- **Tackle Tokenism:** Treat training as part of a broader strategy for reconciliation, not as a box-ticking exercise.
- **Address Resistance:** Create a safe space for participants to confront discomfort, biases, or privilege. Use skilled facilitators to guide these discussions constructively.
- **Foster Organisational Support:** Leadership must champion cultural awareness initiatives, embedding them into organisational culture and policies.

By proactively addressing these challenges, organisations can ensure their cultural awareness programs are impactful and meaningful.

Integrating Training into Organisational Practices

For cultural awareness training to effect real change, it must be embedded into the fabric of an organisation's operations and culture. Training outcomes should inform recruitment, community engagement, and policy development.

Strategies for integration include:

- **Leadership Commitment:** Senior leaders must actively support and model cultural competency.
- **Embedding Practices:** Use training outcomes to shape

organisational policies, ensuring they reflect respect for Aboriginal cultures.

- **Measuring Impact:** Regularly evaluate the effectiveness of training and adapt based on feedback from Aboriginal communities and participants.
- **Enhancing Engagement Skills:** Ensure training content includes practical tools for engagement, such as how to identify stakeholders, respect cultural protocols, and navigate community dynamics effectively.
- **Creating Safe Spaces:** Foster environments where Aboriginal employees and community members feel valued and respected.

Cultural awareness training should also prepare participants to engage with sensitivity and respect, informed by a deeper understanding of the people they are engaging with and the cultural and historical contexts that shape those communities.

What This Means in Practice

Cultural awareness training is a foundational step towards building stronger, more respectful relationships with Aboriginal communities. Effective programs go beyond the surface, addressing historical injustices, systemic inequities, and unconscious biases while equipping participants with the tools to engage meaningfully.

By overcoming challenges and embedding training into organisational practices, organisations can transform their approach to Aboriginal engagement, contributing to lasting reconciliation and mutual respect. When aligned with practical engagement skills, such as identifying stakeholders and understanding cultural practices, these programs become instrumental in fostering trust and collaboration.

Cultural awareness training is not an endpoint but a continuous journey, one that builds the capacity to engage with Aboriginal communities in a way that is informed, respectful, and impactful.

18

The Two-Way Conversation

Moving Beyond Authoritarian Approaches

Traditional engagement methods often rely on authoritarian approaches, imposing decisions on communities without meaningful community involvement. This one-sided method marginalises Aboriginal voices, leaving communities feeling excluded and distrustful of the process.

A two-way conversation shifts this dynamic, fostering mutual respect, collaboration, and shared ownership of outcomes. By treating Aboriginal communities as equal partners, organisations can build trust and ensure engagement reflects the values, priorities, and knowledge of the people they work with. This collaborative approach requires organisations to listen actively, adapt their strategies, and share power in decision-making processes.

Levels of Engagement

Engagement is not a one-size-fits-all process. It exists on a spectrum, with each level suited to different goals and circumstances. The International Association for Public Participation (IAP2) provides a widely recognised framework that outlines five levels of engagement, from basic information-sharing to full community empowerment.

- **Inform:** The goal is to provide stakeholders with accurate and timely information. This is suitable for general updates or awareness campaigns where the primary focus is on keeping stakeholders informed without requiring their input.
  - **Example:** Publishing a newsletter to share updates about a land management project.
- **Consult:** Consulting involves seeking feedback from stakeholders on decisions, analyses, or proposed alternatives. This level of engagement ensures that community voices are heard and considered, but does not necessarily involve shared decision-making.
  - **Example:** Conducting surveys or holding public meetings to gather community input on a new infrastructure project.
- **Involve:** This goes a step further by working directly with stakeholders throughout the process to ensure their concerns and aspirations are consistently understood and integrated.

- **Example:** Hosting workshops with community members to co-develop strategies for preserving cultural heritage sites.

- **Collaborate:** Collaboration involves forming partnerships with stakeholders, giving them an active role in decision-making. At this level, organisations and communities work together to develop alternatives, identify solutions, and implement initiatives.
  - **Example:** Creating a joint task force between a local council and Aboriginal Traditional Owners to manage a protected area.
- **Empower:** Empowerment represents the highest level of engagement, where final decision-making authority is placed in the hands of the community. This level demonstrates the utmost respect for Aboriginal agency and sovereignty.
  - **Example:** Granting Traditional Owners the authority to approve or reject development proposals on their land.

Understanding these levels allows organisations to tailor their engagement strategies appropriately. It also helps manage expectations by clarifying the scope and purpose of each interaction.

Fostering Mutual Learning and Growth

A two-way conversation is not only about consultation; it is an opportunity for mutual learning and growth. Aboriginal communities bring invaluable knowledge of culture, history, and environmental stewardship, while organisations can provide resources, training, and support to empower communities.

To foster mutual learning:

- Encourage open dialogue where both sides share and respect each other's expertise.
- Create environments where cultural and technical knowledge can coexist and complement each other.
- Build capacity within communities to enable greater participation in decision-making processes.

Mutual learning transforms engagement from a transactional process into a relationship-building effort, where both parties grow and benefit from the exchange.

Incorporating Feedback Loops

Feedback loops are essential for maintaining trust and ensuring continuous improvement in engagement practices. These mechanisms allow stakeholders to evaluate the process, highlight areas for improvement, and share insights on their experiences. Effective feedback loops involve:

- **Regular Check-Ins:** Periodic discussions with community representatives to review progress and address concerns.
- **Transparent Communication:** Clearly outlining how feedback will be used and providing updates on its implementation.

- **Adaptability:** Demonstrating a willingness to adjust plans and strategies based on feedback.
- Incorporating feedback loops reinforces the idea that engagement is an ongoing conversation, not a one-time event. It ensures that the process remains aligned with community needs and expectations.

What This Means in Practice

The two-way conversation approach redefines engagement as a collaborative, respectful, and dynamic process. By moving beyond authoritarian methods, adopting the five levels of engagement, fostering mutual learning, and incorporating feedback loops, organisations can build genuine partnerships with Aboriginal communities.

This model empowers communities to shape their futures while equipping organisations to approach engagement with cultural sensitivity and mutual respect. The outcome is a more inclusive, impactful, and sustainable engagement process that reflects the shared wisdom and aspirations of all parties involved.

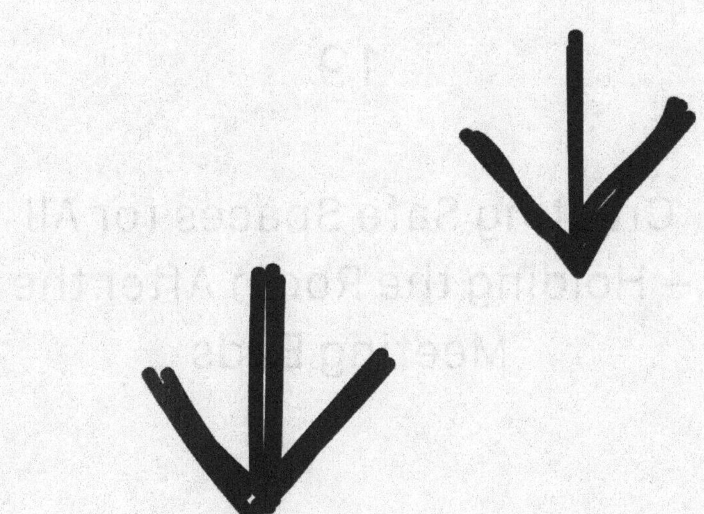

murun

Emu

19

Creating Safe Spaces for All – Holding the Room After the Meeting Ends

Safety Must Be Mutual

In Indigenous engagement work, we often speak of creating a culturally safe space for Aboriginal and Torres Strait Islander participants. This is essential; many come into the room carrying intergenerational trauma, unresolved grief, and a deep frustration from decades of being unheard. But equally important—and less often discussed—is the safety of the other side of the table: the staff, the facilitators, the note takers, and the observers who may be encountering these truths for the very first time.

Cultural safety must be a shared condition, where all voices are respected, but where no one is left overwhelmed or unprepared to process what they've just experienced.

The Room Will Get Heavy

Engagement is not always a tidy or polite exchange. It can become emotional, intense, and at times confrontational. It is not uncommon, nor inappropriate, for Aboriginal participants to express anger, grief, or exhaustion. They may speak about massacres, stolen land, broken promises, or failed Native Title processes. They may use sharp language. They may cry. They may vent.

These moments are not personal attacks. They are the result of generations of systemic harm and are sometimes the only opportunity a community has had to be heard by government staff face-to-face.

But for those on the receiving end, particularly if it's their first time hearing about these lived realities, it can be deeply unsettling. Staff may feel personally responsible, emotionally affected, or unsure of how to respond. If left unaddressed, this emotional toll can create disengagement, resentment, or even trauma among the professionals sent to support the engagement process.

That is why supporting all participants before, during, and after is vital.

Your Role as Cultural Translator and Debrief Facilitator

Recently, I attended an engagement session where a particularly distressed community group raised concerns about the ongoing impacts of colonisation, broken trust, and unresolved land issues. It was heavy, there was pain, raw and historical.

Afterwards, I took time to speak with the government staff and facilitators in the room. I let them decompress. I answered their questions. I didn't minimise what they had heard, but I helped them make sense of it. And it made a difference.

Sometimes people just need a space to say, "That was a lot," and to be reassured that feeling overwhelmed doesn't mean they've failed, it means they've felt something real. That human response can be the beginning of real change.

As engagement leads or cultural consultants, part of our job is to hold that space for everyone. Not just during the meeting, but after.

Practical Ways to Support Both Sides

- **Set the Expectation Early:** Let both the community and government stakeholders know that the space is intended to be honest and respectful, but also emotionally charged at times. Acknowledge that people may react differently, and that's okay.
- **Normalise Emotional Responses:** Whether someone tears up, shuts down, or becomes defensive, remind them that emotional reactions are normal in cross-cultural discussions, especially when truth-telling is involved.
- **Offer a Debrief Session:** After heavy engagements, schedule time to meet with staff or facilitators. This can be a short discussion, either one-on-one or as a group, where you help them:

  - Process what they heard.
  - Understand the cultural and historical context.
  - Ask questions without fear of saying the wrong thing.
  - Reaffirm their purpose in the engagement process.

- **Be Available, But Set Boundaries:** Make yourself available for follow-up conversations, but also set expectations around time and energy. Cultural load affects both Indigenous participants and those supporting them.
- **Use Reflection, Not Just Reporting:** In post-engagement documentation, include space for reflections, not just factual meeting notes. This humanises the process and allows teams to revisit the emotional and relational aspects of what occurred.
- **Remind Everyone Why They're There:** Engagement is not always smooth, and discomfort is not failure. Sometimes it's a sign of progress.

What This Means in Practice: Holding the Room Long After It's Empty

True engagement doesn't end when people walk out of the room. If we want to build trust, shift systems, and truly listen, we must hold space for all the people in the room —those speaking truths and those learning to hear them.

Creating a safe space is not just about emotional protection. It's about mutual care. It's knowing when to speak and when to be silent. It's knowing that both Indigenous and non-Indigenous people are walking out of that room changed, and being prepared to support that change with empathy, patience, and presence.

20

Sitting Fees – Valuing Time, Knowledge, and Cultural Authority

Equity in Practice, Not Just Principle

In the field of Aboriginal engagement, sitting fees are not a token gesture; they are a matter of dignity, equity, and cultural respect. Despite this, many organisations still struggle to understand why Traditional Owners, Elders, and community members should be paid for their time and expertise during consultations or cultural advisory processes.

Let's be clear: sitting fees are payment for services rendered. When Aboriginal people contribute to a meeting, review a document, offer cultural advice, or provide community insight, they are working. Their knowledge, often built over lifetimes and passed down through generations, is a form of intellectual and cultural property and holds immense value.

Would you ask a lawyer to provide free legal advice? Would you expect a professional consultant to offer their expertise without compensation?

Everyone else in the room — project managers, planners, government officers, and engineers — is being paid for their contributions. The same must apply to Aboriginal people. The cultural knowledge and lived experience they bring are just as essential, often more so, to the success and ethical grounding of any engagement process.

The assumption that Aboriginal people should give their time for free stems from a long history of extractive engagement. This mindset must be actively dismantled.

What Are Sitting Fees?

Sitting fees are payments provided to community members for participating in formal engagement processes. These include, but are not limited to:

- Attending consultation meetings or forums.
- Providing cultural advice or feedback.
- Participating in advisory panels or working groups.
- Contributing to policy, planning, or project development.

Sitting fees are not donations or handouts. They acknowledge time, knowledge, and the emotional and cultural labour involved in participation. They respect the fact that engagement comes at a cost — time away from family, community, or Country — and that this contribution deserves fair and timely compensation.

Why Sitting Fees Matter

- **Equity:** If non-Indigenous professionals are paid for their time, Aboriginal contributors must be too. Anything less is discriminatory.
- **Recognition of Expertise:** Cultural knowledge is no less legitimate because it isn't framed in Western academic or bureaucratic terms. It holds equal, if not greater, authority in matters of land, law, language, and community governance.
- **Economic Inclusion:** Paying sitting fees supports economic participation. Many Aboriginal Elders, particularly those on limited incomes, see sitting fees as meaningful contributions to their wellbeing and family responsibilities.
- **Relationship Building:** Offering sitting fees sends a message: We value you. We respect you. We want to do this the right way. It builds trust and helps set the tone for genuine partnerships.

Implementing Sitting Fees Respectfully

- **Be Transparent Upfront:** Clearly state in your invitations or engagement briefs that sitting fees will be offered, including the amount and payment method.
- **Follow Local Norms:** Some communities have standard sitting fee rates. Others align with state or departmental guidelines. Use these as your benchmark and do not undercut or guess at what's appropriate.

- **Where No Local Guidance Exists:** In areas without a recommended sitting fee rate, a fair and transparent approach is to use the local cost of living as a guide, specifically, the median square metre price for residential housing. This reflects the real economic context in which Elders and community members live. It ensures that compensation is not tokenistic and provides a practical, data-driven method for adjusting fees by geography. For example, a project engaging with Elders in a high-cost urban area should not offer the same rate as one operating in a remote region with significantly lower living expenses. Equity means adjusting for these differences.
- **Account for Travel and Preparation:** Sitting fees should reflect not just meeting attendance, but also travel time, cultural preparation, and the role individuals play before and after formal sessions.
- **Pay Promptly:** Delayed payments are not just poor practice; they are disrespectful. Honour your commitment and ensure systems are in place to enable efficient payments.
- **Offer Payment Options:** While cash payments are not permitted in most systems, ensure that bank transfer and invoicing processes are accessible, particularly for Elders. Provide assistance where needed and never place the administrative burden solely on the participant.

Linking Value to Land and Responsibility

Where engagement is tied to land development, planning schemes, or natural resource management, consider aligning sitting fees proportionally. If a project has significant financial or commercial value, it is only right that the contributions of Traditional Owners are compensated in ways that reflect that scale.

This is not about commodifying culture; it's about ensuring that those whose land is being discussed or developed are not the only ones participating without financial return.

What Happens When Sitting Fees Are Not Paid?

- People disengage from the process.
- Communities begin to see consultation as exploitative.
- Trust is eroded.
- Cultural leaders are left to bear the cost of participation.

Failing to pay sitting fees doesn't just impact the individuals; it damages the credibility of the entire engagement process.

What This Means in Practice

Sitting fees are not a favour. They are not optional. They serve as a baseline for respectful, culturally safe, and equitable engagement.

When Aboriginal people are invited to contribute their time, stories, and cultural knowledge, it must be understood that this is professional input, not charity. The old narrative that Aboriginal engagement should happen "from the heart" while everyone else is paid for their work is no longer acceptable.

Everyone at the table is working. Everyone at the table should be paid.

dimunn

camp site

21

Respecting the Clock – Timing and Scheduling with Community

Understanding That Your Calendar Isn't Always the Right One

Time is a man-made construct. It's been structured into calendars, deadlines, and schedules, designed to serve systems, institutions, and economic outcomes. But in Aboriginal communities, time is often experienced differently. It's not measured in boardroom appointments or quarterly targets. It's guided by seasons, stories, obligations, and relationships, not a rigid clock. Time is relational, not transactional. That's why respectful engagement means more than simply showing up on time. It means understanding that your urgency doesn't override someone else's rhythm. What might seem like a delay in an office setting could, in a cultural context, be the correct and necessary pace.

Your Urgency Is Not Their Emergency

Government or project timelines often move quickly. But that pace should never be forced onto the community. Traditional Owners, Elders, and Aboriginal organisations usually have full calendars of commitments, many of which hold far more importance than a stakeholder briefing or survey request. Rushing, pushing, or expecting immediate responses is not only disrespectful, but it's also a recipe for shallow engagement. Instead of saying, "Can we lock in a date next week?" try asking, "Do you already have engagement or meeting days scheduled that we could request a time slot in?" This slight shift acknowledges that you're entering an existing schedule rather than creating one.

Things That Can Affect Community Availability

- **Sorry Business:** Mourning protocols take priority over all other matters. Always ask respectfully if the community is observing Sorry Business before scheduling.
- **Seasonal Weather:** Rain and wet season conditions can cut off roads or limit access to Country, especially in remote or regional areas.
- **Weddings, Festivals, Cultural Events:** Celebrations and ceremonies often follow traditional calendars or family timelines. They take precedence over formal consultations.
- **Limited Internet and Phone Access:** Not all communities have reliable digital connectivity. A delayed

response doesn't mean disinterest—it might just mean no reception.

- **Community Priorities:** Aboriginal organisations are often working with minimal staff and high community demand. Your project might be one of many on their plate.

Build Time into Your Planning

Respectful engagement means starting earlier than you think you need to. Don't leave consultation to the last minute and expect a fast turnaround. Allow at least 2–4 weeks for formal responses. If requesting a presentation or meeting, give plenty of notice and be flexible with your availability. Follow up only after a reasonable time has passed, and never assume silence is consent or disinterest.

Ask First, Don't Assume

Before locking in a date or assuming a communication method, ask:

- "When do you usually hold community or board meetings?"
- "Is there a time of year that's best to talk about this?"
- "What's the best way to send information, email, call, or in person?"
- "Would you prefer a briefing before the engagement process begins?"

This shows respect for both the individual's time and the community's governance process.

Be Prepared to Wait

If you're engaging properly, you'll sometimes need to wait. You'll need to slow down. You may need to stop altogether and come back when the time is right. This isn't a failure of process; it's the process working correctly. Trust built on your timeline isn't real trust. Trust built over time is.

What This Means in Practice

If engagement is going to be meaningful, it must happen on a shared clock—not one dictated solely by project plans or government deadlines. Respect the community's calendar. Ask the right questions. Make time for genuine relationships. Because if the timing isn't right, the engagement won't be either.

Migunn Karulbo

Teach / learn together

PART 4

TOWARDS RECONCILIATION

jagun
place

22

The Evolution of Community Engagement

Understanding the Historical Context

The way organisations engage with Aboriginal communities has evolved significantly over time, shaped by broader societal changes and shifting understandings of cultural respect and inclusion. Historically, engagement efforts often reflected the dominant attitudes of their era, with little consideration for the voices and agency of Aboriginal people. These approaches frequently perpetuated systemic inequities and cultural misunderstandings, leaving communities disempowered.

For example, early government policies treated Aboriginal people as subjects to be managed rather than partners in decision-making. Engagement often consisted of tokenistic consultations or paternalistic initiatives that ignored cultural protocols and community needs. Recognising this historical context is essential for understanding why meaningful, respectful engagement is critical.

Lessons from the Past

Reflecting on past failures provides invaluable insights into how engagement practices can be improved. Key lessons include:

- **Tokenism Harms Relationships:** Engagement efforts that are superficial or symbolic, such as unrepresentative consultations or one-off events, undermine trust and fail to address community concerns.
- **Cultural Competency is Non-Negotiable:** Disregarding Aboriginal cultural practices and values often leads to misunderstandings and disengagement.
- **Representation Matters:** Engagement must involve the right stakeholders, including Elders, Traditional Owners, and other key community representatives, to ensure it reflects the community's true interests.

These lessons highlight the need for intentionality, preparation, and respect in all engagement efforts.

Contemporary Practices and Their Impact

Modern engagement practices represent a shift away from these historical failings. Today, there is a stronger focus on co-design, collaboration, and empowerment. Key elements of this shift include:

- **Shared Decision-Making:** Recognising Aboriginal communities as equal partners in determining outcomes.
- **Long-Term Relationships:** Moving beyond transactional interactions to build ongoing partnerships based on trust and mutual respect.
- **Accountability:** Ensuring that organisations follow through on their commitments and remain transparent about their processes and intentions.

By embracing these principles, contemporary engagement practices seek to repair the harm caused by historical approaches while laying the foundation for reconciliation.

Building a Path Forward

The future of community engagement lies in building genuinely equitable and inclusive partnerships. This involves not only refining engagement strategies but also addressing the systemic barriers that have historically marginalised Aboriginal communities.

To move forward, organisations must:

- **Acknowledge Historical Wrongs:** Begin every engagement effort with an understanding of the historical context and its ongoing impact.
- **Commit to Continuous Improvement:** Regularly evaluate and adapt engagement practices based on community feedback and evolving needs.

- **Invest in Relationships:** Recognise that engagement is not a one-time effort but a continuous process of building trust and collaboration.

What This Means in Practice

While many of the principles of effective engagement have been discussed throughout this book, this chapter highlights the importance of understanding where we have come from to inform where we are going. By reflecting on the evolution of engagement practices and learning from past mistakes, we can ensure that future efforts are more respectful, inclusive, and impactful.

Community engagement is a living practice, shaped by history but not bound by it. Through a commitment to continuous learning and growth, we can build a path toward reconciliation that honours the resilience and wisdom of Aboriginal communities while fostering genuine collaboration.

23

Navigating Institutional Power Imbalances

Protecting Cultural Integrity Within Systemic Structures

When working in engagement roles, particularly within government departments or large corporations, practitioners often face navigating the heavy machinery of institutional power. These environments can bring with them established hierarchies, rigid processes, political agendas, and timelines that are rarely aligned with community priorities or cultural protocols.

This chapter addresses a reality not often openly discussed: the power imbalance between institutions and Aboriginal communities, and the tension that engagement practitioners, especially Aboriginal engagement officers, must navigate as they work within systems that were not designed to serve the communities they now claim to consult.

Understanding Institutional Power

Institutions operate on frameworks built for compliance, efficiency, and control. While those within them may have good intentions, institutional culture often values outputs over outcomes, pace over process, and certainty over community-led change.

These forces can show up in subtle ways:

- Imposing fixed engagement timelines despite community needs.
- Expecting immediate consensus where intergenerational discussions are required.
- Prioritising policy outcomes before trust is established.

For Aboriginal practitioners, the conflict can feel internal. You may be asked to advocate for decisions you disagree with, to soften cultural concerns to fit departmental language, or to justify the need for further consultation when you're already hearing "enough voices."

The Dual Role of the Aboriginal Engagement Practitioner

Engagement workers often walk in two worlds. For Aboriginal practitioners, this can be a double burden:

- Inside institutions, you're expected to represent the community.
- Within community, you may be viewed as representing the system.

Holding these tensions can be emotionally and culturally exhausting. Worse, it can place you in situations where you're either pressured to bend protocols for progress or penalised for protecting cultural integrity.

It's critical to understand that being in the system doesn't mean being of the system. The power of your position lies in the ability to advocate from within. You carry cultural values that systems need, even when they don't understand them.

Strategies for Navigating Power Imbalances

- **Name the Power Structures:** Acknowledge when timelines, project scopes, or budget restrictions are influencing or limiting the engagement process. Speak to it openly in team meetings and internal documents. When power is made visible, it becomes easier to challenge.
- **Protect Cultural Non-Negotiables:** Clearly define what cannot be compromised, whether it's language use, protocols for involving Elders, or the time required for decision-making. Frame these not as preferences but as essential cultural governance practices.
- **Build Internal Allies:** Identify champions inside the institution, leaders, executives, or non-Indigenous staff who are willing to learn and advocate. These allies can amplify your voice when resistance emerges and help hold the line when pressure builds.

- **Document Everything:** Keep records of when advice is given and when it is ignored. This protects you and your integrity, particularly if decisions later create tension with community. It also supports institutional accountability.
- **Use Language Strategically:** Institutions often respond to policy terms more than cultural language. Framing issues in terms like "reputational risk," "compliance breach," or "cultural safety obligations" can help shift internal responses when cultural explanations fall flat.
- **Create Exit Pathways in the Work:** Not every project will unfold ethically. Where possible, build "exit clauses" into the process, clear moments when communities can say no or disengage without penalty. Protecting their sovereignty must remain a priority.

When You Are the Lone Voice

There may be times when you are the only person in the room advocating for cultural integrity. In these moments, remember:

- You are not alone in the broader movement for justice and cultural survival.
- It is not your responsibility to fix the system, but to speak the truth within it.
- Protecting your well-being is as important as protecting the process.

What This Means in Practice

Working within institutions can be a powerful way to create change, but it comes with risks, compromises, and emotional strain. Recognising power imbalances is not about fostering division; it's about protecting the cultural integrity of engagement. True reconciliation requires institutions to meet communities on equal ground. Until that is the norm, those who work inside must act as both translators and guardians of culture, of truth, and of respectful process.

muni

kangaroo

24

Engagement Fatigue and Emotional Labour

The Unseen Costs of Cultural Representation

Engaging with Aboriginal communities is a profoundly human process, one that relies not just on skill and experience but also on presence, empathy, and resilience. For Aboriginal engagement practitioners, especially those working within institutions, this work often demands far more than what is acknowledged in a job description. It draws on cultural, emotional, and spiritual energy, often without adequate support.

This chapter explores the reality of engagement fatigue and emotional labour, particularly for Aboriginal workers who are continually expected to "be cultural," to translate between worlds, and to absorb the weight of systems that still haven't learned how to carry the work respectfully.

Engagement fatigue occurs when individuals or communities are repeatedly asked to give, respond, advise, or participate, without rest, recognition, or adequate compensation. It is especially present in:

- Communities are constantly called upon for consultation without decision-making power.
- Cultural leaders are asked to participate in every meeting, welcome, or endorsement.
- Aboriginal staff are pulled into every project to provide "the cultural input."

The fatigue is not just physical; it is spiritual and cultural. It stems from being seen as a resource rather than as a human being with limits, emotions, and responsibilities beyond the institution.
For Aboriginal practitioners, emotional labour includes:

- Constantly navigating cultural misunderstandings with diplomacy.
- Carrying intergenerational trauma while holding space for others.
- Being the only Aboriginal voice in decision-making rooms.
- Having to educate colleagues while also protecting community integrity.

This labour is often invisible. It doesn't show up in performance reviews, position descriptions, or project scopes, but it is essential to maintaining relationships and cultural safety.

This work is exhausting because:

- You're expected to always represent culture with grace, even when tired, grieving, or disheartened.
- Few organisations have culturally safe supervision, debriefing spaces, or culturally literate leadership.
- Institutions can treat Aboriginal knowledge as something to be accessed on demand, often without rest or replenishment.
- Bridging the gap between government and community puts you in the middle of expectations, tension, and politics.

Protecting your own well-being is not selfish; it is necessary. Boundaries are a form of cultural care.

- Say "not now" when your cup is empty. You are not obligated to attend every meeting or speak at every event.
- Defer when appropriate. Elevate other voices in community or on your team. It doesn't always have to be you.
- Ask for backup. Institutions must build teams, not rely on individuals to carry the cultural load alone.

Institutions must:

- Acknowledge the emotional load in policies, supervision, and workload planning.

- Provide culturally safe debriefing, including access to Aboriginal mentors, Elders, or wellbeing workers—not just standard EAP services.
- Build cultural capability across teams so Aboriginal workers aren't carrying the entire responsibility for cultural integrity.
- Recognise cultural load in remuneration discussions and treat it as a core aspect of leadership and expertise.

Communities also feel this burden. Being asked to show up repeatedly, to give insight, permission, blessing, or critique without seeing change is exhausting.

Meaningful engagement is not constant engagement. Sometimes, the best thing an organisation can do is pause, reflect, and act on what has already been shared.

What This Means in Practice

The emotional labour and engagement fatigue borne by Aboriginal practitioners and communities is real, and it is costing people their health, energy, and joy.

To do this work ethically and sustainably, both individuals and institutions must respect the limits, share the responsibility, and prioritise care.

True engagement honours not only what people bring to the table, but what it costs them to keep showing up.

25

Best Practices for Engagement

Embedding Cultural Overlays from the Start

Embedding **cultural overlays** at the outset of any engagement process is essential for creating meaningful, respectful, and impactful relationships with Aboriginal communities. This requires integrating cultural considerations into every stage of planning, rather than treating them as an afterthought or token addition.

Practical Steps for Embedding Cultural Overlays:

- **Research the Community:** Learn about the specific history, cultural practices, and protocols of the community you are engaging with.
- **Consult Early and Often:** Engage Elders and cultural advisors during the planning phase to ensure alignment with cultural values.

- **Tailor Your Approach:** Adapt engagement strategies to reflect the unique needs of the community, such as scheduling around cultural events or offering interpreters for traditional languages.
- **Use Culturally Appropriate Practices:** Incorporate elements like Welcome to Country ceremonies and traditional meeting structures to show respect and recognition.

Embedding cultural overlays ensures that engagement efforts resonate with the community's values, fostering trust and reducing the risk of misunderstandings.

Recognising Shared Goals

Engagement efforts are most effective when they are built around shared goals. Identifying these goals requires dialogue, mutual respect, and a willingness to adapt to the priorities of Aboriginal communities.

Practical Steps to Identify Shared Goals:

- **Start with Listening:** Conduct listening sessions to understand what matters most to the community.
- **Collaborate on Objectives:** Work together to define goals that benefit both the community and the organisation.
- **Be Transparent About Limitations:** Clearly outline what can realistically be achieved and seek consensus on priorities.

- **Celebrate Common Ground:** Emphasise areas of alignment, such as protecting cultural heritage, improving environmental sustainability, or enhancing community well-being.

Recognising shared goals not only builds stronger relationships but also increases the likelihood of project success by aligning with the interests of all parties involved.

Ensuring Representation and Fairness

Fair representation is a cornerstone of ethical engagement. Aboriginal communities are diverse, with a wide range of perspectives, roles, and responsibilities. Ensuring that all relevant voices are heard requires deliberate and inclusive strategies.

Checklist for Representation and Fairness:

- **Stakeholder Identification:** Have you included Elders, Traditional Owners, youth, and representatives of local organisations?
- **Avoiding Gatekeeping:** Are you engaging with a diverse range of voices rather than relying on a single individual or group?
- **Accessibility:** Have you considered barriers such as language, geography, or scheduling conflicts?
- **Equity in Resources:** Are you providing participants with the same level of information and support to contribute effectively?

Fair representation also involves acknowledging the historical context of power imbalances and working actively to address them. This includes compensating participants for their time and expertise through sitting fees and ensuring that engagement processes are inclusive and transparent.

Tools and Resources for Effective Engagement

To make best practices actionable, consider leveraging the following tools:

- **Engagement Plan Templates:** Create structured plans that outline objectives, stakeholders, timelines, and evaluation methods.
- **Sample Questions for Consultations:** Use thoughtful, open-ended questions to guide discussions, such as:
  - What are the community's top priorities for this project?
  - How can we better align our approach with your cultural values?
- **Cultural Protocol Guides:** Work with cultural advisors to develop guidelines specific to the community you are engaging with.
- **Case Studies:** Review successful examples of Aboriginal engagement to identify strategies that can be adapted to your context.

What This Means in Practice

Best practices for engagement are about more than just principles—they are about action. By embedding cultural overlays, recognising shared goals, ensuring representation and fairness, and using practical tools, organisations can create engagement strategies that are respectful, impactful, and sustainable.

These practices lay the groundwork for meaningful partnerships, allowing organisations and Aboriginal communities to work together toward shared successes. Engagement is not just a process—it is a commitment to equity, mutual respect, and a better future for all.

ngara

gathering

26

Accountability – When You Get It Wrong

Everyone Makes Mistakes

In Indigenous engagement, mistakes are inevitable. Whether it's mispronouncing someone's name, failing to consult the right people, overlooking a protocol, misusing terminology, arriving unprepared, or unintentionally offending someone, at some point, you will get it wrong.

And that's okay.

This work is relational. It's layered. It's embedded in lived experience, history, and cultural responsibility. No one enters this space with perfect knowledge. Aboriginal and Torres Strait Islander engagement is not about following a checklist; it's about building and sustaining relationships. And relationships, by their nature, involve missteps.

What matters most is not whether a mistake is made, but how it is addressed.

True accountability is not about perfection. It's about recognising when harm has occurred, taking responsibility, and working respectfully to repair trust. Accountability, in this context, is not performative. It's relational. It's a practice.

The Real Risk Is Inaction

One of the most common mistakes non-Indigenous practitioners make is not showing up at all. The fear of "getting it wrong" becomes so overwhelming that it leads to avoidance. People don't make the call; they pull out of meetings and stop engaging altogether. They disappear when challenged.

But disengagement is often more damaging than the mistake itself.

Communities notice who shows up and who doesn't. They see who stays in the room when it gets uncomfortable. Walking away to protect your own comfort only reinforces the power imbalance. It places the emotional burden back on Aboriginal people to carry the weight of silence, retreat, and unresolved issues.

Engagement is not about being flawless. It's about being present. Mistakes are part of learning. Integrity is what you build when you stay.

What Accountability Looks Like in Practice

- **Own It Early and Fully.** If you've made a mistake, acknowledge it. Don't wait for someone else to raise it. Don't minimise it. And avoid the temptation to explain your intentions, because intention is not the same as impact.

Say it plainly:

- "I realise I mispronounced your name. I should have asked first."
- "We overlooked an important group in our invitations. That was an error on our part."
- "We went ahead without confirming proper protocol. That was inappropriate."

Avoid defensive language like "I didn't mean to offend" or "That wasn't my intention" — these phrases centre your feelings instead of recognising the harm done.

Accountability means owning the outcome, not explaining it away.

- **Don't Perform the Apology.** An apology is not a performance. It's not a box to tick or a chance to win favour. You are not entitled to immediate forgiveness or restoration of trust. What you are responsible for is the quality of your response.

A good apology is:

- **Short:** No long-winded explanations.
- **Sincere:** Speak plainly and with humility.
- **Specific:** Name what happened, and what you're doing to change it.

Structure it simply:

- Acknowledge the harm.
- Accept responsibility.
- Outline how it will be prevented in future.

Then step back and let your actions speak for themselves.

- **Learn and Apply the Lesson:** A genuine apology leads to behavioural change. Reflect on what went wrong, but go deeper, ask what systems, assumptions, or blind spots contributed to the mistake. Who was excluded? What questions weren't asked? What knowledge was missing?

Then, act.

- Update your protocols.
- Change your process.
- Review who is in the room and who's not.
- Build mechanisms for cultural safety before mistakes occur, not after.

Learning without action is just performance. Accountability means putting the lesson to work.

- **Stay in Relationship** Mistakes strain relationships, but they don't have to break them. Many Aboriginal people are used to people coming in and out, making promises, and vanishing when it gets hard. You rebuild trust by staying consistent.

Don't ghost the process.

Keep showing up, not with defensiveness, but with humility. Acknowledge that trust is not yours to demand; it's yours to earn.

Cultural Safety Is a Shared Responsibility

Too often, Aboriginal people are left to carry the emotional burden of correcting others. They are expected to absorb the harm, do the education, and continue to engage without support. This dynamic is neither fair nor sustainable.

Accountability means shifting that weight.

- Step in when you witness harm.
- Correct your colleagues.
- Hold your own team to account.
- Don't wait for an Elder or community member to say something; be proactive.

Cultural safety doesn't come from one person in a team; it's a shared, ongoing responsibility. And it starts with being prepared to get it wrong, take the hit, and still stay in the work.

A Story: Getting It Wrong and Making It Right

There was a time I introduced a Traditional Owner using a name that had been anglicised in an old report. I repeated that name during a formal engagement without first confirming it with him. In front of the group, he corrected me. He was respectful, but I could tell he was disappointed.

After the meeting, I approached him directly. I apologised, acknowledged the mistake, and committed to correcting the materials going forward. I didn't explain it away; I just owned it. Later, I followed through by ensuring the correct name appeared in all documents and presentations. I made sure others on the project did the same.

Weeks later, another community member quietly said to me, "You owned that. That matters."

That moment didn't damage the relationship. If anything, it strengthened it. Not because I got it right, but because I was willing to get it right after getting it wrong.

What This Means in Practice: Accountability Is Respect in Action

You will get it wrong at times; that's just a fact, and that's okay.

Accountability is not about perfection. It's about how you respond when mistakes happen. It's about listening, taking responsibility, and showing that your commitment to this work is bigger than your ego, your role, or your comfort.

Accountability is respect in action.

It shows that you're not here for optics. You're here for truth. You're here for a relationship. You're here to learn and to keep showing up.

And in this work, that matters more than always getting it right.

What This Means in Practice: Towards Meaningful Engagement

Reflection on the Journey of Engagement

The process of engaging with Aboriginal communities is a journey, not a destination. It requires patience, humility, and a willingness to unlearn old ways of thinking while embracing new ones. Throughout this book, we have explored the multifaceted aspects of engagement, from understanding history and identity to fostering genuine partnerships built on trust and respect.

This journey has taught us that engagement is more than a set of tasks or a box-ticking exercise. It is an ongoing relationship that values dialogue over directive, learning over assumption, and collaboration over control. The principles outlined in this book serve as a guide to navigate the complexities of working alongside Aboriginal communities, but they are not static rules. Each engagement is unique, shaped by context, people, and purpose.

Building a Future of Respect and Collaboration

As we look toward the future, the importance of respectful and meaningful engagement becomes even more pronounced. The path to reconciliation and equity is paved with genuine partnerships that honour the voices, knowledge, and leadership of Aboriginal communities.

To build this future:

- **Centre Aboriginal Voices:** Ensure that Aboriginal communities are not only consulted but actively lead decisions that impact their lives and lands.
- **Foster Shared Ownership:** Collaborate to define goals, strategies, and outcomes, ensuring that all parties feel invested and valued.
- **Commit to Continuous Learning:** Recognise that cultural competency and respectful engagement are

lifelong processes that require ongoing reflection and growth.

- **Advocate for Structural Change:** Use your influence to address systemic barriers and support policies that empower Aboriginal communities and promote equity.

The journey of engagement is a two-way street. Just as we learn from Aboriginal communities, we must also share our knowledge, resources, and networks to create a foundation for mutual growth and understanding. This reciprocity is the heart of meaningful engagement.

A Call to Action

The principles in this book are only as powerful as the actions they inspire. Whether you are a government official, a corporate leader, a community organiser, or an individual seeking to make a difference, the responsibility lies with each of us to apply these lessons thoughtfully and consistently.

Engagement is not about perfection; it is about progress. It is about showing up, listening, and being willing to adapt when needed. It is about respecting the past, understanding the present, and working together to build a future that celebrates the richness and resilience of Aboriginal culture and community.

Together, we can move beyond performative gestures and create authentic, equitable, and enduring relationships. This is the essence of meaningful engagement, and it is the legacy we should all strive to leave behind.

Practical Resources and Appendices

Tools to Support Respectful and Effective Engagement

This section provides tools, templates, and reference materials to help readers apply the principles outlined in this guide. These resources are intended for individuals and organisations seeking to strengthen their engagement practices with Aboriginal communities.

Stakeholder Mapping Template

Effective engagement starts with knowing who to engage and how to reach them. The template below can be used to map Traditional Owners, Elders, knowledge keepers, community groups, and organisations relevant to your project.

Contact Name	Area	Position/ Title	Organisation	Phone	Email	Notes	PBC	Claim Group
John Doe	SEQ	Director	QAFNQBC	5550 9876	John@ QAFNQBC. com	Meeting set for Monday	YES	QAFNQ BC PBC

Use this tool in the early stages of planning. Revisit and update it regularly, especially when working across regions or on long-term projects.

Sitting Fee Guideline Reference

Sitting fees are a minimum standard for valuing the time, knowledge, and presence of Aboriginal participants. They must be discussed early and paid promptly.

Recommended Practice:

- Use rates aligned with local Aboriginal land councils, cultural bodies, or state government guidance.
- Ensure the rate reflects time, travel, preparation, and cultural contribution.
- Avoid flat token amounts—compensate according to the scale and complexity of engagement.
- Payments should be made via bank transfer (cash is discouraged due to compliance rules).
- Provide a point of contact for assistance with paperwork and follow-up.

Glossary of Respectful Engagement Terms

This glossary includes terms frequently used in engagement and how to use them correctly:

- **Traditional Owner:** An Aboriginal person with ancestral ties and responsibilities to specific land or waters.
- **First Nations:** A collective term recognising the sovereignty of all Aboriginal and Torres Strait Islander peoples.
- **Elder:** A respected person in the community acknowledged for cultural wisdom and guidance. Not all older people are Elders.
- **Knowledge Keeper:** A person responsible for preserving and transmitting specific cultural knowledge, which may not be shared widely.

- **Cultural Protocols:** Accepted practices that govern respectful interaction with Aboriginal communities, including who to speak with, how, and when.
- **Sorry Business:** A period of mourning observed in Aboriginal communities. Engagement must pause during this time.

Always check the preferred local terms and their meanings with the community you are engaging with.

Do's and Don'ts for New Staff in Engagement Roles

A simple reference to help new team members understand the expectations of working respectfully in Aboriginal engagement settings.

Do:

- Do your homework learn the history of the people and place you're engaging with.
- Listen more than you speak.
- Be transparent about your role and intentions.
- Offer sitting fees and confirm them early.
- Acknowledge limitations in your knowledge, seek guidance.
- Follow up with communities and close the loop.

Don't:

- Don't assume one person can speak for the whole community.

- Don't use acronyms or jargon without explanation.
- Don't push timelines that don't suit the community.
- Don't treat cultural contributions as free labour.
- Don't rush silence, it can be part of the process.
- Don't engage only when it suits the project, build genuine relationships.

Walking in Two Worlds

Respectful engagement is not about perfection—it is about intention, consistency, and accountability. These tools are provided to support your journey, but they are not a substitute for relationships. Go slow. Ask questions. And above all, let the community guide the way.

Jimbelung

Friend / ally; relationship-first connection

About the Author

Shannon Best is a respected Aboriginal leader, artist, and engagement specialist with deep cultural ties to the Yugambeh region of Southeast Queensland. As the General Manager of the Yugambeh Museum and First Nations Engagement Lead in regional planning for the Queensland Government, Shannon works at the intersection of cultural heritage, policy, and community development.

He has led groundbreaking engagement projects across multiple sectors—including infrastructure, water planning, arts, and heritage—ensuring Traditional Owners and Elders are meaningfully involved in decision-making. Shannon is also the founder of several successful global businesses, a two-time world champion athlete, and a three-time Hall of Fame inductee.

With decades of experience navigating institutions and advocating for cultural integrity, Shannon brings a lived understanding of the challenges and responsibilities of Indigenous engagement. His work continues to influence policy, uplift community voices, and guide organisations across Australia toward more ethical and authentic relationships with Aboriginal people.

More Big Sky Books

www.bigskypublishing.com.au

If you would like to share your views on this book or other Big Sky titles please post a review or drop us an email!

You can follow our pages to see more about our books, or post your own review on Big Sky Publishing's Social Media accounts: